Management

THE ART OF WORKING
WITH AND THROUGH PEOPLE

MANAGEMENT

The Art of Working
With and Through People

DONALD C. MOSLEY
University of South Alabama

PAUL H. PIETRI, JR.
Mississippi State University

Dickenson Publishing Company, Inc.

Encino, California

Dedicated to our parents

ISBN-0-8221-0137-8
Library of Congress Catalog Card Number: 74-79427

Printed in the United States of America
Printing (last digit): 9 8 7 6 5 4 3 2 1

Contents

Two Definitions of Management: Administrative and Operative   Four Functions of Management: Planning, Controlling, Organizing, Supervising   What a Manager Does
Summary   Questions

The Growth of an Organization: Four Stages   Unity of
Command and Span of Control: Two Important Management
Principles   Conflicts Between Line and Staff People and
Between Departments   How to Avoid Excessive Con-
flict: Delineating Authority   Summary   Questions
Notes

Planning: The Primary Function of Management   Controlling: The Complement to Planning   Summary
Questions   Notes

PART 2   OPERATIVE MANAGEMENT   45

Preface

Not long ago we were asked to recommend a book on operative management for a management-development program for middle-level and first-line supervisors. About the same time we were asked to recommend a text for a community-college beginning management course. In neither case did we know of a suitable book.

That is why we wrote *Management: The Art of Working With and Through People*. It is mainly designed to help develop the supervising, motivating, and communicating aspects of working with and through people so as to achieve effective results. These are the things that supervisors and managers on the firing line are most concerned about. These are the things that make or break not only a supervisor but in many cases the organization itself.

The book is also intended to provide you with a frame of reference for understanding the organizational environment you are or will be working in. The major focus is on first-line and middle management. But you will be made acquainted with the important principles of planning, organizing, and controlling, with how an organization grows and develops, how higher level managers function, what top management expects from operating managers, and what the future trends in management are. We hope these ideas will not only enable the manager to gain self-growth and development, but also to create an environment where his employees can grow and develop. This should, in turn, enable him and his organization to gain more effective results.

We have written the book without prerequisites in mind, so that the student and practicing manager can begin study right away. We have tried to make the writing style easy to follow and have used numerous examples throughout. As a special feature we present, at the end of the book, cases and role-playing situations corresponding to the concepts and principles described in the chapters. These were developed from our management consulting experiences and will allow you to practice management under simulated conditions.

We are indebted to our many friends, both teachers and students, who indirectly contributed to this book. We are especially indebted also to the practicing managers in manufacturing companies, banks, hospitals, government agencies, and educational institutions throughout the country with whom we have worked in past years. Finally, we would like to thank the Bureau of Business and Economic Research at Mississippi State University for providing assistance with typing the manuscript.

D.C.M.
P.H.P.

Management

THE ART OF WORKING
WITH AND THROUGH PEOPLE

Part 1

A Management Framework

1

What Management Is: A Process That Makes Things Happen

We predict you will find this book both interesting and worth-while. We make this prediction not because of anything special that we have done but because the subject of management itself is so dynamic, interesting, and worthwhile. In fact, in a free-enterprise, capitalistic society, managers practicing good management are a most important resource, for they determine to a large extent the economic well-being of three major groups—employees, stockholders, and customers. Whether the society and individual businesses within it realize their potential economic growth and development depends on the type of management practiced.

John W. Gardner has stated that there are three keys to an organization's success: effective leadership, effective recruitment of people, and the effective development of people. Note how he emphasizes leadership and development of people. He goes on to point out that a business organization is similar to a civilization: it may have a long life cycle or a short one, and during this cycle it may level off in growth, become stagnated and decline, or blossom forth and go on to achieve new heights of success and growth. Again, effective or ineffective leadership, effective or ineffective development of people, will primarily determine which way the organization will go. Thus to a large extent leadership and the development of people is what much of management is all about.

TWO DEFINITIONS OF MANAGEMENT: ADMINISTRATIVE AND OPERATIVE

Management is not easy to define, perhaps because so many different people and disciplines have an interest in the field. Still, some definitions stand out and two may be used as working definitions. *Administrative management* is the planning, organizing, and controlling of the activities of a business so that they are coordinated in the attainment of the business objectives. *Operative management* is the supervising, motivating, and communicating aspects of working with people to achieve effective results. The higher a person is in a business organization, the more he is concerned with administrative management and the less with operative management. And the lower the position he holds, the more he is concerned with operative management. No management is exclusively either operative or administrative, but has elements of both. Figure 1 shows the relationship between them.

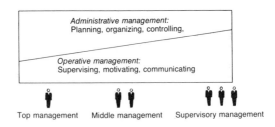

Figure 1. People in the lower levels of management spend proportionately more time directly supervising and working through their subordinates so as to meet the goals of higher management. People in the higher levels spend more time in determining policy, setting goals and budgets, and making long-range forecasts.

FOUR FUNCTIONS OF MANAGEMENT:
PLANNING, CONTROLLING, ORGANIZING, SUPERVISING

The definition of management functions is likewise difficult because there is no general agreement on them. However, most activities of management, we believe, can be included under the four functions of planning, controlling, organizing, and supervising, although there is considerable overlap among them.

Planning, which some management experts believe a manager must engage in first before he can do anything else, is concerned with setting goals and objectives and determining ways of reaching them. Plans take many forms, including establishing policies, procedures, projects, budgets, standards, forecasts, strategies, and deadlines.

Controlling is concerned with ways of making happen what was planned to happen. Control presupposes the existence of plans: a person does not control in the abstract but controls against a standard or plan. Sometimes both planning and control are reflected in the same tools, such as budgets, deadlines, sales quotas, and production or cost standards.

Organizing is concerned with deciding on what activities are needed to attain company objectives, with establishing the relationships betwteen these activities, and with staffing people to perform them. Organizing is a continuing process, a means to an end, and although a well-designed organizational structure will not ensure success, it will make the odds greater. The next chapter explores this function in some depth, since an insight into organizing will help you better understand what follows in the rest of the book. Chapter 3 examines the functions of planning and controlling.

Supervising is primarily operative management. People in their first management jobs are expected to devote a large amount of time to this function, and should continue this emphasis as they move into middle management. To supervise is simply to motivate people to do their jobs efficiently so as to achieve effective results. This requires leadership in the form of instructing, communicating, counseling, disciplining, and developing people. Most of this book emphasizes this function in order to give you the insights and know-how to become an effective operating manager. Top managers are also concerned with supervision and leadership, though it differs somewhat from that of operating managers.

WHAT A MANAGER DOES

As the cake-like illustration in Figure 2 shows, the four management functions are like four layers, and are common to different types of management, as represented by the six slices of the cake. The four layers represent what a manager should do, and it makes no difference whether he is a plant manager, an insurance executive, or a military commander. Although a first-line supervisor will be more concerned with supervision, at times he will be involved in planning, organizing, and controlling. On the other hand, if he operates a lathe during a rush period, it is not a management activity, nor is it if an office manager types a report or a sales manager engages in direct selling.

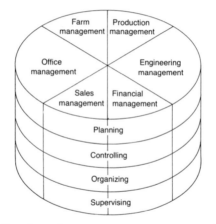

Figure 2. The four functions of management are common to all types of management.

SUMMARY

This chapter presented two working definitions which we will observe for the rest of the book. It also demonstrated that all management activity falls into one of the four functions—planning, organizing, controlling, and supervising. We pointed out that the first-line supervisor is engaged in carrying out management functions just as is the company president. However, the president is more concerned with administrative management, whereas the first-line supervisors and middle-level managers spend more time on operative management.

QUESTIONS

1. Explain the difference between administrative management and operative management. Explain their relationship to the management structure in the business organization. Do they exist separately? Do they overlap? What elements compose each?

2. Identify the four management functions. How do they relate to a specific manager's job? Do you think someone versed in these management functions can perform satisfactorily in any management position?

2

Organization:
Calling Others in to Help

An understanding of organizational theory and the organizing function is most important for anyone in an organization, whether industry, government, military, or church, who aspires to a managerial position. If he does not understand the organizing function, it may lead to many problems and prevent the organization from realizing its objectives. Examples of problems that could develop are:

—Failure of managers to understand the company as a whole because of involvement with one department.

—Excessive violation of the unity of command principle.

—Improper development of additional departments when needed and assignment of duties and responsibilities to new employees.

—Inefficient use and development of personnel because of improper delegation of authority.

—Excessive and unhealthy conflicts between departments and between line managers and staff personnel.

In this chapter, we will try to give you some initial insights into how to deal with these and other problems and provide you with a framework for understanding the following chapters.

THE GROWTH OF AN ORGANIZATION: FOUR STAGES

To see the organizing function of management in operation, let us study the growth and development of a hypothetical manufacturing company.

Stage 1: A One-Man Business in a Garage

Our story begins in 1960 in a small Midwestern city of 75,000. Our main character is John Moody, 29, a high school graduate and Korean war veteran who has been working in a large paper mill by the river on the outskirts of the city since his discharge from the service in 1954. John still holds the same semiskilled job at the operative level that he originally started with, and his wife's relatives believe he is a lazy person with a low IQ who will never amount to much. Actually, John is quite an intelligent person, but his basic satisfaction in life comes from the challenge of building and creating things in his garage workshop. Although he believes he will never get rich, he feels his take-home pay is sufficient to take care of the necessities of life and to support his hobbies. Even though his job at the mill is not very challenging, he gets all the challenge he needs from tinkering around in his workshop.

Unfortunately, in early 1960, the country begins to slide into an economic recession, which has an adverse effect on the paper industry. Several mill employees, including John, are laid off because of excessive inventory build-up. John signs up for unemployment compensation and decides to spend time building a new boat trailer in his garage. He puts a lot of thought and effort into the task, and as a result builds an excellent boat trailer—such a fine one, in fact, that several of his friends talk him into building boat trailers for them at expenses plus a 20 percent markup. Even at this price his boat trailer sells for less than those sold in local stores, and before long, so many requests are coming in that John finds himself spending all his time in his garage.

At this point John decides to work full time building boat trailers as long as he can make a living doing so. He is now in the first stage of business growth: as Figure 3 shows, he is a one-man operation financing, producing, and selling a product—the three basic activities common to all manufacturing companies.

Figure 3. Stage 1: John Moody decides to go into the manufacturing business.

Stage 2: The Owner-Manager and His Assistants

After three months John finds so many orders are coming in that he cannot fill them. In the past few years the federal government has built a number of dams near John's town, creating four new lakes in the region. Fishing has been good, and so there has been a large demand for boats and boat trailers. John is now making more money per day than he did when he was with the mill. To keep pace with the orders, he hires Ray Martin, a former army buddy, to help build the trailers, and for a small monthly salary his wife agrees to keep books and handle the financial details. Before the month is out, Ray has mastered his job so well that he and John are producing more boat trailers than they have orders for.

At this point John and Ray start thinking about someone they can hire as a salesman. As it turns out, Ray's brother, Paul, has just graduated from college with a major in marketing. Because his grades were not very good, he has had trouble finding a job. After being approached by John and Ray, he decides the company has possibilities, and with the assurance of an opportunity to buy into the company in the future, he starts to work as a salesman. As a result of growth, the business has now moved fully into stage 2: as Figure 4 shows, John has had to call in others to help carry out

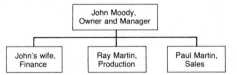

Figure 4. Stage 2: Business has grown so that John has had to hire a person to help him in each major area.

the three primary activities of the company. Many companies skip stage 1 entirely and begin with stage 2 by initially hiring a manager and assistants. This period is a critical time, since over 50 percent of new businesses fail in their first year of operation—from lack of capital, ineffective management, or both.

Paul proves to be an excellent salesman and the business continues to grow. To keep up with the increasing volume of orders, John then hires additional people and the company moves to a larger building. As Figure 5 shows, after two years, the

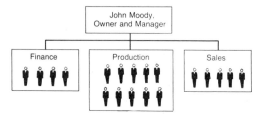

Figure 5. Stage 2: After two years, there are four people in finance, ten in production and five in sales—and John is about to work himself to death.

company has grown so that John has nineteen people working for him. His net income is such that his wife has quit working, but John finds himself so busy he cannot enjoy his higher income. More important, he feels he is losing control of the business, and increased costs per boat trailer support this belief.

In desperation John calls in the Martin brothers to solicit their ideas about his dilemma. Paul recalls that in one of his college courses students talked about the *span of control principle* of management. This principle holds that there is a limit to the number of people a manager can effectively supervise. In Paul's opinion the solution to the problem is to select managers for the areas of finance, production, and sales.

Stage 3: The Line Organization

This solution seems so simple that John wonders why he did not think of it himself. Accordingly, he places Sam Fields, his best accountant, in charge of finance, Ray in charge of production, and Paul in charge of sales. At this point, the company moves into stage 3 of organizational growth: as Figure 6 shows, the company is in a line structure and managers have been selected for the three major departments. John now has a span of control of three rather than nineteen, and he finds time to concentrate more on such things as developing plans for the future, coordinating the work of the three departments, and supervising his managers.

As a result of the new organization and the capabilities of the managers, the cost of making each boat trailer (the unit cost) is

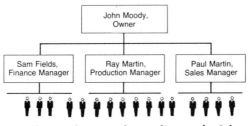

Figure 6. Stage 3: Following the span of control principle, John names a manager in charge of each area.

lowered. Under the leadership of sales manager Paul Martin, the company expands its sales territory to cover most of the states in the Midwest. As sales increase, production also increases, and so new people are added in both sales and production; thus, the organizational structure develops to accompany the increased growth. Keeping in mind the span of control principle, John adds new sections in production and sales whenever the volume of business justifies the new additions.

During this period of growth the company is evolving solely as a *line organization;* that is, the three departments are concerned with the primary purpose of the business, which, of course, is manufacturing and selling a product. Thus, the growth of the company is occurring in the line areas of production and sales. There are three advantages to being in a line organization at an early stage of the company's growth. First, because authority is so centralized—it is in the hands of John and his three managers— quick, decisive action on problems is possible. Second, lines of authority are clearly defined and each person is accountable to his immediate superior; he looks to him for orders and for direction, evaluation, and control of his performance. Third, in a pure line organization everyone knows what his job is and what his obligations are. As a result, there is a minimum of evasion of responsibility and accountability.

After ten years the company is employing over 700 people. During this period, John has elevated Ray Martin to production manager over five production department heads; as Figure 7 shows, this move creates an additional level of management in the production division. The department heads in turn are each responsible for four foremen, each supervising ten production workers. Similarly, John has made Paul Martin sales manager in charge of three regional sales managers, each supervising eight salesmen.

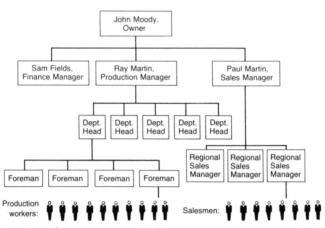

Figure 7. Stage 3: As business grows, the line-organization structure develops to enable John Moody to maintain control.

Stage 4: The Line-Staff Organization

Unfortunately, increasing sales require the company to add additional people in order to meet production quotas, and so the profit on each unit produced declines. Finally, Sam Fields, the head of finance reports to John that each $1 in sales is costing $1.10. In other words, a boat trailer that the company sells for $200 is costing $220 to manufacture. Although the company is now sound financially, John is aware that the way things are going it will not take long to go bankrupt. He therefore decides to call in a reputable management consultant.

The consultant interviews managers from different levels in the company, and after several days of investigation, he makes the following report to John Moody.

My investigation reveals there has been a common mistake that many companies make: You are operating purely as a line organization, whereas at your stage of growth you need to move into a *line-staff* structure. You will need to hire several staff experts and take away some of the activities your line managers presently have. As it stands now, your organizational structure and way of operating tend to overload your managers; they are in effect wearing too many hats. More specifically, I have found the following three kinds of evidence of inefficiency:

—Your supervisors are doing their own hiring, firing, disciplining, etc. Consequently, you have no uniform way of screening, selecting, promoting, and disciplining employees. Moreover, I have found evidence that a number of the supervisors are hiring friends and relatives for their departments, and other employees believe favoritism is rampant throughout the company.

—The several department heads independently purchase materials and supplies for their departments. This duplication of effort has resulted in excessive space and dollars tied up in raw material inventory. In addition, this practice has opened the door for waste and pilferage of supplies and materials.

—Your department heads and supervisors are involved in method and layout studies, maintenance and repair work, scheduling and dispatching, and, to cap it off, quality control—all of these activities are in addition to their primary jobs of supervising the work and motivating their men. The old proverb that a jack of all trades is a master of none is certainly borne out by the situation I find in your plant.

My primary recommendation, therefore, is that you hire a personnel manager to screen, select, and train employees, a production and inventory control manager to do all the purchasing, and an industrial engineering manager to do method and layout studies and the like. (Their relationship to the organization is shown in Figure 8.) By adding these three staff specialists, you will give your department heads and supervisors a chance to really do their primary job of overseeing production and motivating their men. Equally important, you should receive immediate benefits and cost savings by eliminating inefficiencies and installing improved ways of operating as a result of hiring staff experts.

The consultant went on to report that in the future additional staff people would be needed if the company continued its rate of growth. He also stated that in the future it might want to consider diversification by adding additional product lines that would require similar skills. The John Moody company accepted the consultant's recommendations of becoming a line-staff organization and went on to achieve not only record sales but record profits and

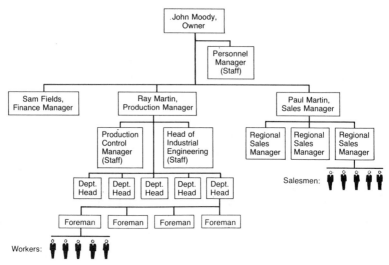

Figure 8. Stage 4: The line organization becomes a line-staff organization, with the addition of three staff specialists who are experts in their fields.

growth. Ultimately, any growing company needs to pass into this fourth stage; unfortunately, some do not and so suffer the consequences—usually decline and bankruptcy.

UNITY OF COMMAND AND SPAN OF CONTROL: TWO IMPORTANT MANAGEMENT PRINCIPLES

Let us now discuss two principles that are particularly applicable to the organizing function of management and to the art of working with and through people to achieve objectives.

The *unity of command principle* goes like this: Everyone in an organization should report to and be accountable to only one boss.[1] This superior is responsible for evaluating their performance, for passing down orders and information, and for developing subordinates as employees of the organization. It is to him that subordinates should turn to for help in carrying out their duties and for communicating any deviations, either positive or negative, in implementing their duties. In sum, the superior is the one responsible for motivating his employees to achieve effective results and for taking action when subordinates deviate from planned performance.

Adherence to the unity of command principle is important for five reasons. First, it prevents duplication and conflict when orders and instructions are passed down. Second, it decreases confusion and buck-passing, for everyone has one boss and knows he is accountable to him; the organization can also hold the boss accountable. Third, it provides a basis whereby a superior and his subordinates can develop a real understanding of what is expected of each other and a knowledge of each other's strengths and weaknesses. Fourth, it provides an opportunity so that superior and subordinates may develop supportive relationships and so realize their individual and group potential in achieving organizational objectives. Finally, it promotes higher morale than is generally found in organizations that do not follow the unity of command.

Unfortunately, some managers only give lip service to this principle, although their organization chart may prefer to reflect it. Recently one of the authors was working with a branch plant of a blue-chip corporation to tailor a management-development program, and among other things, was examining the leadership styles practiced by key managers and their effect on subordinates. To determine these leadership styles, managers at all levels were interviewed. The results showed that the plant manager, though unusually capable and generally effective in managing, made one mistake with his subordinate managers: he violated the unity of command principle in that he periodically conducted inspections throughout the plant and made on-the-spot suggestions to operative employees. Often times, these suggestions were made when the employee's superior was not present. As a result, operative employees were following instructions that their immediate superiors were unaware of. Moreover, the employees would stop working on their assigned duties in order to carry out the instructions of the plant manager. As a result of this one error, a morale problem had developed and many of the effective managerial practices of the plant manager were being undermined. When this situation was called to the plant manager's attention, he was quite surprised. It seems that he had slipped into this habit without being fully aware of its long-range consequences. This manager thereupon began passing his suggestions and instructions through his subordinate managers, and as a result morale improved.

Although employees should have only one superior, they may, of course, have relationships with many people. For example, in an organization that has moved to the line-staff stage of organization growth, line supervisors and department heads will have many contacts with staff personnel. These contacts are necessary so that both line and staff personnel can accomplish their duties. Later in this chapter we will explain how these relationships can be developed without violating the unity of command principle. The important thing to remember is that if there should be a conflict between a staff request and a line manager's command, the subordinate should have a single superior he can turn to for clarification or a final decision.

As we illustrated with the growth of John Moody's company, sooner or later the number of subordinates reporting to one superior will grow to exceed his control. This *span of control principle* is very important, and because the thinking about it has changed over the years, we will examine it in detail. Before World War II, experts maintained the span of control should be three to eight persons, depending on the level of management. Thus, in those days one of the first things an organizational consultant examined when a company was having problems was the span of control at various levels. Today this does not hold as true, and we have defined the span of control principle simply as this: there is a limit to the number of people a person can effectively manage. Just as a man can span only a limited number of feet and inches with his arm, so his mental reach can span only a limited number of problems, situations, and relationships that make up the activities of management. Actually, the span of control will vary depending on the type of organization, the amount of coordination required, and the level of management. One thing we can say without qualification is that as one moves down the ladder from administrative management to operative management, the span should increase.

Why is it that the higher a manager is in an organization the smaller should be the number of people who report directly to him and vice versa? There are four primary reasons. First, administrative leadership requires the ability to solve a variety of different, nonrecurring problems and requires much mental concentration on problems. Second, higher level managers must spend much of their time in long-range planning, working with outside interest groups and coordinating the various activities of the business. They cannot afford to be tied down by the excessive burden of supervision that comes when a large number of people report directly to them. Third, operative managers, by contrast, tend to be concerned with more clearly defined areas of operation. Fourth, although operative managers will be responsible for a certain amount of coordination with other departments, most of their contacts are directly with their immediate subordinates. Thus, they are able to supervise more people than higher level managers.

Companies that follow a policy of a narrow span of control are often hampered in achieving effective results. A large organization of, say, a thousand people that rigidly adheres to a span between three and seven will have a tall, narrow organizational structure (with many, many management levels), which will cause some disadvantages. More supervisors will be required, resulting in higher payroll costs. Communication must pass up and down through many levels, causing greater possibility of distortion. The danger of oversupervision may lead to the curbing of decision-making by subordinates and so curb the opportunity to develop their potential. The only advantage of tight control is that the work can be closely directed, so the company can hire relatively lower skilled people.

Over the years, then, many companies have tended to broaden their span of control at all levels. There are at least three reasons for this trend. First, higher educational attainment, management and supervisory development programs, vocational and technical training, and generally increased knowledge on the part of the labor force have increased the abilities and capacities of both superiors and subordinates. And it is a well-known fact that the greater the capacity of the superior the greater his ability in supervising more people. Second, research indicates that in many situations general supervision is more effective than close supervision. General supervision permits supervision of more people, and a wide span of control forces more general supervision. Third, new developments in management permit us to broaden the span of control and supervise by results without losing control. By using a computer, for example, an organization can process information faster and develop more efficient business reporting systems.

CONFLICTS BETWEEN LINE AND STAFF PEOPLE AND BETWEEN DEPARTMENTS

As we stated earlier, line personnel carry out the primary activities of the business—the producing or selling products or services—whereas staff personnel assist the line people and aid top management in planning, organizing, controlling, and supervising. Line units, then, are like the main stream and staff units are like the tributaries serving and assisting the main stream, although they should not be thought of as being secondary to the line units. Both are important.

Once a company has reached the fourth stage of growth and is no longer a small business, it becomes more complex and difficult to coordinate. A line-staff structure that places experts in certain positions will help eliminate confusion, duplication, and inefficiencies, but it will not solve all problems for all time: a growing organization must continually be alert to pitfalls and potential trouble spots.

One common problem area is excessive conflict between line and staff personnel and between different departments. Some differences in viewpoint between people and departments are, of course, natural, inevitable, and healthy, but excessive conflict can disrupt an entire organization and prevent the achievement of otherwise obtainable objectives.

There are at least six reasons why excessive conflict can develop within an organization. First, many people in staff departments—industrial engineering, production control, quality control, cost accounting, and personnel—have to work closely with line managers. Occasionally their work takes them directly to the production floor and as a result they may get beyond their area of responsibility and in effect pass out direct orders to line personnel. Second, many times for many reasons, both staff and line personnel neglect to use common sense and good human relations when dealing with one another. For instance, line personnel may resent the staff person because he is a college graduate and wears a white shirt; staff people may resent line people because they are not more cooperative in helping implement pet staff ideas.

Third, conflict may arise because people do not know where the authority and responsibility of one department ends and another begins or where responsibilities overlap. Fourth, line people may feel that staff personnel simply do not understand what is going on at the operating level. Fifth, top management may misuse or fail to use staff personnel. For example, if a company has a highly paid personnel director, but top management never solicits his views about employee turnover, instead always turning to the production manager, this could cause resentment and frustration. On the other hand, if top management used staff personnel to check on things all over the plant and gave the personnel manager broad, sweeping powers to make decisions and pass out orders, all sorts of conflicts and tensions could result.

The sixth and final reason for conflict is that each department often sees the entire plant in terms of its own department. When this happens, members of a department fail to see that the duties and responsibilities of other departments are equally as important as their own to the achievement of objectives—indeed, sometimes departments will actually be working at cross purposes.

HOW TO AVOID EXCESSIVE CONFLICT: DELINEATING AUTHORITY

One way to avoid excessive conflicts in an organization is to have effective communications between people and between departments, a topic we will take up in Chapters 7 and 8. At this point we will only point out that key managers overseeing both line and staff people can improve the communication process by periodically bringing together line and staff people to discuss problems that cut across departmental lines. This example may also inspire lower level managers to do the same thing with their key subordinates, and so the danger of seeing only part of the picture will be minimized.

Another major way to avoid potential conflicts is to have people clearly understand the authority-responsibility relationships between individuals and departments. To show this, let us examine the three types of authority.

The Three Types of Authority

The primary responsibility of most staff units is to serve and advise the line. This type of authority is called *advisory* or the *authority of ideas*. However, some staff men may be so zealous in trying to sell their ideas to line personnel that they in effect pass out orders. When this happens, and if the line manager permits it to occur frequently, the unity of command begins to break down.

The second type of authority, called *line authority*, is concerned with the power to directly command or exact performance from others. As we shall see when we study leadership, this power of command does not mean that effective performance results simply from passing out orders and telling people what to do. It means that when one has line authority he is directly responsible for the results of a certain department or group of men. Line authority should not be equated solely with line units. A staff department head would also have line authority over those who report to him in the staff department.

The third type, called *functional authority*, is usually set up as a restricted kind of line authority. For instance, when staff people help top management carry out the managerial functions, the plant manager gives the quality-control staff person the responsibility for controlling the quality of production. However, if everyone knows the extent and limits of the quality-control inspector's responsibility, no problems should result. Under functional authority, the quality-control inspector can only *check* the quality of production; he does not have the authority to *order* production workers to help him in his work. Even if the quality-control inspector pulls a number of units out of production, the line supervisor has the right to appeal to a higher level.

Some other examples where functional authority might be granted to staff specialists by top management might be as follows: (1) A personnel manager has authority to recruit, test, and screen all prospective new production workers for the company. (2) A safety specialist has authority to have chemical departments closed when he feels that fumes in the work area reach an unsafe level. (3) An accounting manager has authority to direct that all plant production managers furnish him with certain cost data at weekly intervals. (4) A public relations specialist has authority to approve and edit all speeches given by company officials.

Functional authority is necessary, but it can be dangerous if it is passed around indiscriminately. Normally, it is given only to a staff area where there is a great deal of expertise and the staff expert's advice would be followed anyway.

Delegation of Authority

One of the most significant facets of management is the process by which a manager allocates authority and responsibility downward to the people who report to him. When the same process occurs for an organization as a whole, with managerial authority being allocated downward to different organizational levels, it is called *decentralization*. It is important to note that after a manager delegates, he is still accountable for the good or bad results of his subordinates' efforts.

We believe that more potentially able managers and supervisors fail in their positions because of their inability to delegate than for any other single reason. As an illustration, one of the authors served in the airborne infantry with a captain who had graduated from West Point. This officer had many excellent characteristics for being an effective leader; he was conscientious and energetic and had a fine mind. However, his unit was considered the poorest in the regiment, even though the captain spent fourteen to sixteen hours each day trying to carry out his duties. Actually, the large number of hours he spent on the job were symptomatic not of inefficient troops or officers but of his inability to delegate. When he attempted to delegate, he would destroy the effect of his action by constantly checking to see if things were going properly and in general breathing down the necks of the people to whom he had supposedly given authority. Consequently, his officers and noncommissioned officers were continually frustrated in using their own ideas and methods and thus took the position, "Well, let's not worry about it, because if we attempt to do anything, he will probably change what we do."

Industrialist Andrew Carnegie once said, "When a man realizes he can call others in to help him do a job better than he can do alone, he has taken a big step in his life."[2] In the formative years of your lives most of your success in school work and on summer jobs depends primarily on your individual efforts. Achievement and success usually do not come from how well you can inspire and develop teamwork and how well you can work with and through people. Then, all of a sudden, you leave school, and after working awhile you are placed in a leadership position. Now instead of having two or three things to be responsible for, you are responsible for working with and through people to accomplish numerous assignments. Perhaps as the new supervisor you can accomplish any one or two activities better than anyone under your command; but can you possibly do all things as well? Unfortunately, many supervisors apparently think they can, because they either fail to delegate or, like the captain, they destroy the effects of delegation by oversupervision.

Why do some managers have so much difficulty in delegating authority? As we already indicated, their previous experience in nonleadership positions sometimes gives them a mistaken notion of how a manager should be. In addition, since a manager is accountable for what his people do or do not accomplish, it is natural to want to stay on top of everything that happens, although it invariably causes resentment in the people supervised.

One management book also lists the following reasons why many managers have difficulty delegating.[3]

1. Some leaders just do not trust people. They are afraid if they don't stay on top of things, the subordinate will do just as little as possible.
2. Some leaders are afraid subordinates will make mistakes. It is a well-known law of learning, however, that people learn best when they are given assignments where they can learn from their mistakes.
3. Some people for psychological reasons have an excessive tendency to dominate people and things. We sometimes see this tendency in mothers rearing their children where the typical product is a mamma's boy.
4. Some managers do not delegate because they are afraid their subordinates will do so well that they will be recognized and promoted ahead of the manager.
5. Finally, some managers honestly assess their subordinates as not having the ability or knowledge to adequately handle responsibilities without close supervision. This situation usually occurs with new employees and on projects calling for an unusual amount of technical knowledge. Yet even in these situations, the wise manager will attempt to develop the abilities of his subordinates so that over time he can delegate more freely and occupy his time with managerial responsibilities rather than close supervision of subordinates.

The above list is not complete, of course. See if you can add to it, drawing from your experience in working with and for various supervisors and managers.

SUMMARY

Organization theory is a rapidly changing, evolving area that draws from many disciplines, but in this chapter we focused on concepts especially relevant to operative managers. We presented several phases of organizational growth and highlighted several important management principles. We also pinpointed some issues in organization life that can make or break operative managers—issues such as conflicts between departments and between line and staff units. Finally, we showed how the attitude and philosophy a manager has toward delegation of authority will dramatically affect his success in working with and through people.

QUESTIONS

1. Outline the four stages of organizational growth and relate them to an organization you are familiar with.
2. What two important management principles affect the successful operation of a growing organization? Do you think John Moody's difficulties could have been avoided had he understood these principles?
3. What is the relationship between organizational structure and management span of control? Consider the advantages and disadvantages.
4. Distinguish between line and staff functions. Are they always easily identified in various types of business enterprises? Justify the importance of both line and staff units.
5. What conflicts may arise between line and staff personnel? What reasons can you give for these problems? How does effective communications ease the conflict?
6. What are the three types of authority? Do they all exist in all four stages of functional growth? Do certain types of authority endanger the unity of command?
7. It has been said that authority can be delegated, but responsibility cannot. Is this a true statement? Clarify its meaning.
8. Briefly present some primary reasons why managers have difficulty delegating authority to their subordinates.

NOTES

1. In some complex organizations, an acceptable violation of the unity of command principle is what is known as a *matrix organization*. This form of organization indicates that a number of organization members may work on special projects as well as in their functional areas. For the life of the project they have two bosses—the project director and the functional department head. An example would be a college professor who teaches in the management department and works half time on an interdisciplinary project.
2. Quoted in George R. Terry, *Principles of Management*, 5th ed. (Homewood, Ill.: Richard D. Irwin, 1968), p. 399.
3. *Ibid.*, pp. 302–303.

3

Planning and Controlling:
The Siamese Twins
of Management

As we noted, the functions of management are planning, organizing, supervising, and controlling. This is also the sequence in which a manager typically performs. First, he comes up with a *plan,* such as a way to reduce the cost of his product. Then, since certain actions must be taken in order to accomplish the plan, the manager must *organize* human effort, including delegating the authority necessary to accomplish the plan. He must then *supervise* his subordinates in their carrying out the plan. Finally, he must exercise *control* to ensure that the results are as anticipated.

It is hard to imagine a manager performing the other functions well without first devoting some time to planning. He must have certain goals in mind before he can assign jobs or projects to his subordinates, supervise them, or control the results. But if any two functions are closely united, they are planning and controlling, and so we shall discuss them together. Since you are already familiar with some of the organizational concepts discussed in Chapter 2, we now think that you are in a better position to appreciate the role that planning and controlling play.

PLANNING: THE PRIMARY FUNCTION OF MANAGEMENT

Simply stated, planning means deciding what shall be done in the future. Planning is looking forward. It takes a certain amount of discipline to plan, since planning is an intellectual process. Because planning must take place before the other functions of organizing, supervising, and controlling, it can be called the *primary* function of management. Planning, then, is a mental process that eventually leads to making decisions about courses of action to take in the future.

To illustrate planning, suppose you and some friends decide to take a weekend camping trip. To plan for the trip, you must resolve some questions. First, where should you go? (How far can you go in a weekend? What camp sites are available? What services are offered at each site? What activities do you have in mind—fishing, swimming, hiking, boating, etc.?) Second, what equipment and supplies will you need? (Tent, sleeping bags, folding chairs, lamps, cooking equipment, tools? What food will you take?) Third, how much should you budget for the trip? (For gas, food, supplies, fishing, etc.?)

This list is not complete, of course—other considerations must be included in the plan (for example, the weather forecast). But note the answers to some questions depend on the answers to the first one, where you will go. Thus, some plans have an impact upon others and vice-versa.

Good planning also anticipates future problems and contingencies. You do not want to arrive at the camp site, set up camp, prepare for the evening meal—and then find you have forgotten to bring a lantern, candles, or flashlight. What, also, if it should rain all weekend? Do you have cards, games, or other activities for indoors? What if all camp sites are taken? Are there others nearby? Are you prepared to rough it in the woods? Should you have reserved a campsite in advance? Obviously, the smoothness of the trip greatly depends on the quality of the planning preceding it.

Similarly, when a retail store anticipates the last week of Christmas shoppers, careful planning is necessary. Will the store stay open at night? Will additional personnel be needed to handle the extra sales, giftwrapping, and delivery service? How much inventory should be carried? Because of the large crowds, can anything be done to provide greater aisle space or easier movement for customers?

Unity of Purpose in Planning

Every organization should have an overall objective or objectives to strive toward. These broad overall objectives are determined by top management, and the efforts of other levels are geared toward reaching these objectives. As Figure 9 shows, a "funneling" type of activity happens.

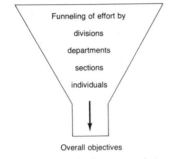

Figure 9. Funneling of effort toward the objective.

Let us assume that President John Moody and his key managers at the boat-trailer company have set sales and profit objectives for the coming year at 15,000 units (boat trailers) and a net profit of $150,000. The personnel, sales, finance, and production divisions will each reflect these overall objectives in its own way. The goals of the production division, for example, will be to produce a trailer that costs less to manufacture and to increase the division's capacity so it can produce 15,000 units. Within the production division, the various departments will each reflect the division's goal. The machining department and assembly department will have specific goals for quality, output, absenteeism and turnover, scrap and waste materials, and so on. The maintenance department will have goals that seek to reduce production time lost by machine breakdowns and malfunctions. The industrial engineering department will have specific goals that will improve production methods and techniques. Departments within the sales, personnel, and finance divisions will also each have their own goals, which in turn contribute to the divisional goals. Finally, the efforts of individual employees in accomplishing their job objectives all contribute toward their departmental goals. The result, shown in Figure 10, illustrates the intermeshing of objectives, or plans, at various levels throughout the organization.

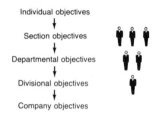

Individual objectives
↓
Section objectives
↓
Departmental objectives
↓
Divisional objectives
↓
Company objectives

Figure 10. The hierarchy of objectives.

To take a slightly different example, imagine that the top management of the Southwestern Badgers, a new professional football team, has just had an important planning meeting. The owner, the vice-president of player personnel, the general manager, and the board of directors, have met and determined that their basic objective will be to build from the bottom up and try to develop into championship contenders in five years. Fans in the community are football-hungry, and it is felt that they will support the team well, despite the first few lean years. Now let us observe how this objective becomes reflected throughout the entire organization.

First, the head coach will realize that if he wins only a few games in the first two seasons, he will not necessarily be out of a job. He will be expected to use younger players, who may make many mistakes but who will gain experience for the longer run. The director of player personnel will reflect the overall objective of building for the future by how he trades and drafts players. When the team limit of forty players is reached, the coaches will be inclined to release older players. Given a choice between the younger, mistake-prone but high-potential rookie quarterback and the older, experienced veteran who may have greater ability, the coach may see that the younger quarterback logs more playing time. Moreover, the public relations department will trumpet the objective loudly and clearly so that hometown supporters will not be overoptimistic in the initial seasons. We thus see the importance of coordination and unity in planning. The overall objectives are determined, and objectives and plans of lower levels reflect the overall plans.

Do All Managers Need to Plan?

Is planning important only to top managers, engineers, or planning specialists? Planning is certainly part of administrative management; however, remember that all managers, regardless of their level, perform both administrative and operative management.

Let us assume that supervisor Anderson, an operative level manager in the Moody Company, has just been handed a number of items produced in his department that were rejected by the quality-control inspection department. "It's that Williams again," Anderson thinks. "He has developed a bad habit of rushing through his welding operation and doing some sloppy welds." Anderson realizes he will have to show Williams the rejects and discuss the problem with him, for such poor performance must be corrected, but what can he do or say that will have the best effect? Will Williams respond best to a chewing out or should he be given a chance to explain? Is he resentful because he did not receive one of the new welding machines just distributed in the department, or is there some other reason? What approach would most likely motivate him to do better work?

In this case, supervisor Anderson is practicing *administrative* management; clearly, he is planning for his future discussion with Williams. But within the discussion, when attempting to communicate with Williams—to motivate him and to gain a better mutual understanding—he is practicing *operative* management. Note how the two go hand in hand. Although, as we stated, higher level managers spend more time on administrative management (planning, organizing, and controlling), this does not mean that lower level managers have no need to perform these functions. On the contrary, planning is important for all managers, regardless of level.

The magnitude and nature of planning does, however, differ at various levels, as Figure 11 shows. While top managers— including company directors, the president, and vice-presidents— spend time planning such things as mergers, rate of growth, and long-run and yearly company objectives, lower level managers plan different things. As one first-line supervisor in a manufacturing company told it, "Planning? Sure I spend time planning. But most of my department's goals, objectives, work assignments, schedules are handed down from above. So my planning is more

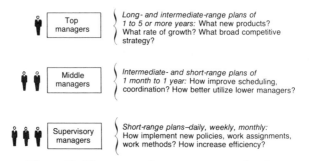

Figure 11. Planning at three management levels.

along the line of: how can I cut down on the turnover and absenteeism rate in my department? how can I cut material waste and
scrappage? given my department's schedule for the week or for
the day, what's the best way to attack it? I plan all right, and it's
important. Last week, for instance, our shift was changed around a
bit and I had a lot of planning to do figuring who'd work where and
when. Things seemed to go a lot more smoothly because I'd put
in some time anticipating the problems."

Thus, all managers need to plan, regardless of their position in
the hierarchy. But planning at top levels is, of course, much more
complex, involves much more uncertainty, and is more highly
critical for the organization as a whole.

Tendency to Slight Planning

Poor planning often produces activities that are disorganized and
uncoordinated and unexpected problems, resulting in lost time,
manpower, and money. As we said earlier, planning is largely a
mental process, and since thinking is often more difficult than
doing, many managers have a tendency to slight planning. It is
usually tempting to forego thinking about the future in order to
concentrate on solving present work problems.

Consider some evidences of poor planning by John Moody
as his business grew from a one-man operation to an organization
of 400 employees. In stage 2, when after two years the company
had grown to twenty people, Moody found himself so busy he
could not enjoy his higher income and, more importantly, felt
he was losing control of the business because of the increased costs
per boat trailer. And in stage 3, the management consultant reported that the company had made the common mistake of

operating as a line organization whereas it should have a line-staff organizational structure. Of course, Moody eventually recognized his weaknesses and took corrective action, but better planning would have produced a more efficient transition into each stage of growth.

As many managers do, John Moody probably had a strong tendency to be too involved in the daily activities of his business. As a result, the planning function suffered. It is not unusual at all for a manager to spend his day "fighting one fire after another," seemingly never caught up in his work. Consider the case of this manager:

Today, I've got four people who didn't show up for work, and my department is absolutely swamped. I'm helping out some, but I've also got to show some staff people from the home office around the production facilities. Moreover, one of my men has been feuding with the maintenance people who he claims are giving other machinists preferential treatment. I've promised to discuss that with the maintenance people today. To cap it off, Alders wants a transfer out of the department and wants to talk about it with me. Then, this afternoon I've gotta have those figures ready for the folks in cost accounting. And on top of all this, I'm supposed to supervise my twenty-five men. What a day! But they all seem to be like this.

Is it any wonder that this manager would forego planning if his typical daily schedule is so demanding? Perhaps not. But ironically, many of the short-run crises that confront a manager can be greatly eased by proper planning. When a manager devotes too little time to planning, it results in any number of short-run problems—including such things as impossible deadlines, unforeseen obstacles, crises, and crash programs. These preoccupy the manager's time, leaving him little time to devote to planning. . . . and the cycle goes on.

Recently, a number of books have been published that deal with "the management of time."[1] In presenting helpful hints on time-saving habits, they suggest that the manager start by first carefully analyzing how he spends his typical day. What part is spent on nonmanagerial activities? What work could be delegated to subordinates? What reports could a subordinate do that the manager presently spends time doing? We have seen many managers who are overworked and seemingly never caught up in their job. Some of these cases have resulted from poor organizing by top management, such as too large a span of management, or having to wear too many hats in addition to responsibility for daily supervision. But many result from the manager's failure to delegate. Regardless of the cause, however, it is the amount of and quality of planning that is likely to suffer. We tend to slight the future to accomplish the present.

Types of Plans: Single-Use and Repeat-Use

Let us now look at several common plans that organizations use. Some are *single-use plans,* used for a given period of time or for a given purpose and then discarded, frequently to be replaced by another plan. Budgets are a popular form of single-use plan; once the budget period expires, a new budget replaces the old one. Other plans are *standing plans* or *repeat-use plans,* which are used over and over again to help guide the behavior of organizational members. Objectives, policies, rules, procedures, and strategies are common examples of standing plans, and we shall describe them below.

Objectives. Objectives spell out ends or goals to be accomplished. Why is Moody in business? Does he want to achieve a target growth rate? Does he want his business to be only boat trailers? Objectives provide the rationale behind effort. Note this broad statement of objectives by a large pharmaceutical company:

1. To earn an adequate return on invested capital through service in medicine.
2. To seek growth in the fields of specialty, nutritional, and pharmaceutical products.
3. To achieve growth through fundamental research and sound product development of the kind and quality designed to contribute to the advancement of medicine and public welfare.
4. Continuously to discover, attract, develop, and properly recognize talent at all levels in order to anticipate and meet the changing needs of business.
5. To provide formal training for all employees to promote individual growth and development.

6. To maintain a high level of employee morale through continuous sound leadership and administration.
7. To discharge the obligation of corporate citizenship by effective participation in and contribution to industry, national, state, and local affairs.

Most businesses have in their "company creeds" or statements of objectives references to stockholders, consumers, employees, the community, and society. Others may include groups such as suppliers, their industry, and the government. As you see from the above statement of objectives, objectives tell *what* it is the organization is after but do not tell *how* it will be accomplished. Subordinate level plans are established to specify the "how."

Divisions, departments, and individual organization members all have specific objectives. As they achieve their objectives, they also contribute to the broader overall organizational objectives.

Policies. Organizations, especially larger ones, need certain guidelines to keep the whole team pulling together. Policies are important in guiding the behavior of managers and other organization members. Generally, policies help tell *how* objectives will be accomplished. For example:

PURCHASING POLICY: We shall have several sources of supply so as not to be totally reliant on only one.

WAGE POLICY: Wages shall be established and maintained on a level favorable to that found for similar positions within our industry and the community.

MARKETING POLICY: Only a limited number of dealers will be selected to distribute and sell the company's product lines in a given territory.

HIRING POLICY: We are an equal opportunity employer.

SUPERVISORY POLICY: Managers should periodically hold group meetings with subordinates for the purpose of discussing objectives of the department, discussing new developments which may be of interest to or may affect subordinates, answering questions, and in general encouraging more effective and accurate communications within the organization.

PROMOTION POLICY: We encourage promotion from within.

A policy may be generally defined as a guide to thinking. It does not give specific answers, but has a certain broadness that helps guide managers and organization members in making their decisions and determining their behavior.

Assume you are a plant superintendent and one of your subordinate managers had just left the company unexpectedly. How would you go about filling the position? If your company had a promotion policy such as the last one in the list above, you would certainly have a guide to help you. But you would not have a crutch, for the promotion policy does not tell you which person to promote. In fact, it does not say that you *have* to promote someone from within the company, only that you should perhaps first look within the departmental ranks for a replacement. And though you should seriously consider an internal promotion to fill the position if no qualified individuals are available, you may still hire someone from outside the company and operate within company policy.

Organizations usually have a number of policies that serve as guidelines for their members. In larger organizations these are usually in writing. In the Moody Company's first two stages of growth, there was little need for formal written policies, but later, when several levels of hierarchy were introduced, the need became greater. Some unwritten or implied policies, however, are just as evident as if they were written. If, over the years, Sultan Oil starts its new sales trainees out pumping gas in a service station, this procedure may not be in writing, but it is an implied policy; it guides a manager's thinking. It does not tell him where to start the new man (what station) or how long to keep him there. But it still qualifies as a policy, and marketing managers may recognize it just as if it were formally written in the company's policy manual.

Rules. A rule, like a policy, also provides guidance. It is stronger than a policy in that the guidance it gives is final and definite. Rules are inflexible: "No smoking allowed on premises"—if you work in the machining department, you cannot smoke, and that is that. A policy would be: "Employees who violate the no smoking rule are *subject* to discharge." A rule would be: "Employees who violate the no smoking rule are *automatically* discharged."

Why distinguish between rules and policies, especially when the line is sometimes such a fine one? First, a manager must know where he has and does not have flexibility. Second, too many rules can result in "overmanagement"; taking too much discretion from a manager leads him to take the attitude of "Well, let me look in the rule book and see what I must do." Under such a situation, managers lose their individualism and may use rules as crutches. Or there may be weak, apologetic enforcement of rules. ("Bill, I'm sorry I have to write you up for punching in three minutes late." "But you know I was actually here twenty minutes early, and just forgot to punch in. I can't afford to get laid off half a day for being written up." "Sorry, Bill, I know it doesn't seem fair, but I've got to stick by the rule book.") We do not mean to imply that rules have no place in organizations, of course, only that their overuse can lead to problems.

Procedures. A procedure spells out steps to be performed. Organizations have procedures on such matters as obtaining leaves of absence, ordering parts through central purchasing, and conducting disciplinary interviews in unionized companies. Procedures provide uniformity of action through a standardized sequence. For example, a company might require that when a salesman writes up a bill of sale, a copy first goes to the credit department for approval, another to production scheduling for an estimated completion date, another to accounting where the sale will be recorded, and a final copy to shipping.

Strategies. Strategies also are repeat-use plans in that they are usually carefully decided upon from a choice of alternatives. Strategies may really overlap policies. When a company has a policy of selling at discount prices, this certainly qualifies as a type of "strategy." And when a large clothing manufacturer allows only one retail store in each city to represent its clothing line, this also seems to be policy and strategy.

Some strategies, however, may be single-use plans. One large company the writers are familiar with anticipated the escalation of the Vietnam war in the late 1960s and followed a strategy of deliberately overhiring college graduates on the premise that large numbers of them would be called into service. They were, and the hiring strategy was successful, for the company was able to continue its expansion uninterrupted.

The single-use strategies that receive most attention, perhaps, are competitive strategies. The automobile industry, for example, constantly has strategic battles being fought. Ford's Mustang, Maverick, and Pinto were parts of a planned market strategy to beat General Motors and Chrysler to the punch in competing with Volkswagen for the sub compact car market. Product strategies, advertising strategies, pricing strategies, packaging strategies, and others play a critical role in the free-enterprise system.

Budgets. Budgets are not only control devices, they are also single-use plans. Budgets are forecasts of expected performance over a period of time. A sales budget refers to sales targets, a financial budget projects spending allowances, a capital expenditure budget sets forth an amount to be spent on machinery and equipment. It is apparent, then, that exceeding some budgets is desirable—as with a sales budget or a units-per-man-hour budget—and exceeding others is undesirable, such as expense budgets, customer return-merchandise budgets, or allowance for bad debt budgets.

Ideally, managers at all levels should be involved in helping arrive at budgets, rather than simply be given a budget by staff groups or top management without any consultation. A manager will more likely be committed to a budget figure that he himself has had a hand in developing. As one manager of a large truck maintenance and repair firm stated:

> Our budget system for a job works like this. A truck comes in and a man in the estimating department figures what it'll take in terms of parts and man-hours work. Next, he'll discuss the figure with me, and we arrive at an estimate based on our markup. I like this system a lot better than the old system. There I was just given a job and told to do it in so many man-hours. Half the estimates seemed unrealistic, and we lost a lot of money on overruns. It wasn't my fault, and I couldn't see pushing my men unfairly. Under our new system, if there's a cost overrun, I feel responsible, and I don't mind it as much when the boss gets on me about it. I still don't like having to explain overruns, but at least now I'm not getting blamed unfairly.

Unlike objectives, policies, rules, and procedures, budgets are discarded when the period of time covered by the budget period is completed.

We hope these sections have given you some insight into the crucial role that good planning plays. But planning by itself cannot do the job. Thus, let us now examine the other Siamese twin of management—controlling.

CONTROLLING: THE COMPLEMENT TO PLANNING

Have you ever driven a car on a highway you were unfamiliar with and come to an unmarked fork in the road? You pulled out your highway map only to find that the fork was not shown. You then chose one route and drove miles and miles before you found a marker that confirmed you took the right road. Managers in many organizations suffer a similar dilemma: they go along not knowing whether they are on the right road or not. Unfortunately, many find they are headed in the wrong direction, too late to do much about it. They do not have the advantage of periodic road markers along the way because they haven't established any. Such road markers might be thought of as control points that help tell you whether you are moving in the right direction.

Controlling complements planning. Planning sets a plane's course and controlling keeps the plane there. When the navigator establishes that the plane is off course, he takes corrective action by having the pilot make some adjustments, otherwise, locating the landing area on schedule would depend largely on luck. Some managers lay out careful and elaborate plans, but unless they employ effective control, accomplishing the plans becomes largely a matter of luck. Perhaps you have heard of Murphy's Law—"If anything goes wrong, it will"—which appears on bulletin boards in all types of organizations. (Variations are: "If several things can go wrong, the one that will go wrong is the one that will do the worst damage." "There's never time to do it right, but always time to do it over." "Once a job is fouled up, anything done to improve it only makes it worse." "Left to themselves, things always go from bad to worse.") Thus, you might think of good control as trying to combat Murphy's Law.

Basically, the control process involves these steps:
—Establishing standards or goals (planning)
—Measuring performance
—Comparing performance with standards
—Analyzing deviations or variances
—Taking remedial action, if necessary (even modifying the original standards)

Controlling, then, cannot take place unless some type of plan first exists. If no standard is set, how can a manager evaluate performance? What guides will he have for remedial action? He cannot really take corrective action, for as soon as he did it would imply he had some standard in mind. Controlling might also lead to modification in the original plans. Sometimes a manager might find performance results differ greatly from the standard established, indicating that the standard was not adequate to realistically test performance or that conditions changed since the standard was set.

Forward-Looking Nature of Control

Although controlling involves measurement of past results, the important phase of it is distinctly done with an eye to the future. For example, suppose that a quality-control inspector in a garment factory finds that in a batch of shirts one sleeve is longer than the other. The labor cost of producing the shirts has already been incurred. Perhaps some or all of the material in the shirts will be scrapped. The forward-looking nature of control comes into play when the inspector asks: "What caused this?" "What can prevent it from happening in the future?" "What action should be taken?"

The decision about where to locate control points must look forward also. If you give one of your workers an important job to finish in one day and find at the end of the day that he did it improperly, you are exercising control too late—you should have exercised it earlier in the day, when you could have caught the errors and taken corrective action. Likewise, if we consider John Moody's goal of selling 15,000 boat trailers the next year, Moody must determine at what points during the year control over sales will take place. If control is exercised only at the end of the tenth and twelfth months and performance falls below expectations, it will undoubtedly be too late to make the necessary corrections in performance and still accomplish the sales goal. In fact, if the only times sales figures are assembled is at the end of the year, then there will be no chance for control to take place. On the other hand, if Moody and his sales managers evaluate and analyze sales figures every month, then if the first month's sales figures dip much lower than anticipated, there is still time to investigate the causes, take corrective action, and possibly still reach the sales goal at the year's end.

What about control over sales daily or even hourly? We do not mean to suggest that a manager should constantly spend his time looking over his subordinates' shoulders. Control costs time and money. Hourly control over sales would mean Moody's salesmen would have to report hourly to their regional managers, taking away time from everyone's other duties, including selling. The question is, considering the costs involved in controlling, how often should control be exercised? In addition, people seem to resent extra tight controls. Subordinates generally like some freedom in their jobs and dislike being controlled too closely (a point we will discuss in detail in Chapter 5); they perceive over-control as representing a lack of confidence in their ability. Thus, a number of factors dictate the amount and closeness of control a manager exercises, including whether the work easily lends itself to control; the experience, training, and skill of the subordinate; the size of the manager's span of control; the costs involved; and the importance and complexity of the work involved.

The Principle of Management by Exception

The control principle of management by exception is "a system of identification and communication that signals the manager when his attention is needed; conversely, it remains silent when his attention is not required."[2] Management by exception allows the manager to concentrate his time and efforts on *important* problems or opportunities that require his attention. In a sense, it involves delegation of authority as well as controlling. As an example, let us assume that John Moody has set a January sales target of 400 boat trailers, or 100 trailers per week. Here's how management by exception would work. As long as weekly sales are between 90 and 110 units, or some other limits felt to be relatively ordinary, Moody need not become concerned about stepping into the picture, and so could concentrate his effort on matters other than sales control. However, if sales deviate from target by more than 10 percent in a particular week, this would be considered an exceptional, nonordinary deviation from standard, and Moody would look more deeply into the matter, finding out causes and planning corrective action. Thus, under management by exception, Moody concerns himself only with *exceptional* departures from standards.

We should note that if sales for one week in January jumped

above 110 units, Moody would also become involved. He would want to know what caused this *exceptional* jump in sales (whether from a special sales contest, changed advertising approach, good weather, or whatever). Moody would want this information if he managed by exception, but so long as performance fell within a 10 percent deviation from standards, his sales manager would have authority to act without Moody's intervention.

Management by exception can be practiced in sales, production, finance, personnel, purchasing, inventory control, engineering, and other departments. Even first-line supervisors can use this principle in their daily supervision.

Problems in Measuring Performance

To control an activity, a manager must have some relatively accurate measure of performance. Some performance can be measured in numerical terms. Budgets, for instance, are forecasts of future performance expressed numerically in units, hours, dollars, or other means. Performance in some position lends itself more easily to this type of measurement than to others. A head coach's won-lost record is there for everyone to see. So is a salesman's sales performance, and so is a machine operator's output. However, there is usually more involved in measuring performance than just playing a numbers game. Should we also measure the coach's human-relations effort, his recruiting of good assistant coaches, his relations with alumni? Is not the salesman's ability to cooperate and take instructions, to be willing to spend nonprofitable selling time developing new territories, also important? But how would you measure numerically or objectively the performance of a secretary or an accountant or a vice-president of personnel? Unfortunately, numerical measurements are not easily available for all types of positions.

For this reason numbers should not be the only measurement of performance used in controlling. Moreover, profit pictures are in themselves sometimes misleading. Suppose that you were the regional manager in charge of four branch stores with the following profit figures for a six-month period:

Store A	$ 6,900
Store B	-1,200
Store C	4,600
Store D	11,300

Which individual store manager has done the best job? Before you make a decision, let us look at the rest of the picture in the table.

	6 Mo. Sales (budgeted)	6 Mo. Sales (actual)	6 Mo. Profit (budgeted)	6 Mo. Profit (actual)
Store A	$ 62,000	$ 71,000	$ 6,000	$ 6,900
Store B	38,000	41,000	2,000	1,200
Store C	53,000	55,000	4,500	4,600
Store D	194,000	128,000	19,400	11,300

While it would appear that store B has done poorly and store D has done best, when we examine the *standards* set, we find otherwise. This is the danger in using only profits as a basis for measurement. What about other numerical standards, such as employee turnover? Profit as a percentage of sales? Losses on bad debts? Profit and sales as a percentage of money invested in each store? There are also the problems of measuring other aspects of performance that cannot be converted to numbers. How about the store's image in each community? What about employee morale? While it is always simpler to set standards for and to measure things that are easily counted, it is also important to develop standards and measurements for nonquantifiable aspects of performance.

SUMMARY

This chapter described two of the four management functions— planning and controlling, the "Siamese twins" of management. Planning, the primary management function, involves setting broad targets or objectives for the future and establishing lower level plans to help reach these goals. Controlling attempts to measure periodically how effectively the plans have been accomplished so that, where necessary, corrective action can be taken.

QUESTIONS

1. Explain why planning and controlling are called the Siamese twins of management.
2. Evaluate this statement by the president of a large furniture company. "Planning? I'm not really worried about planning in our company. I've carefully built up an excellent group of the brightest minds in our industry and put them in charge of all planning for the company. This gives our lower

managers the valuable time they need doing what they're supposed to be doing—supervising their workers. Everybody knows these managers don't have time to plan if they're doing their jobs of good supervision."

3. Discuss how a head football coach exercises control over the performance of his players.

4. Explain how the management by exception principle might be used by each of the following managers:

a. A branch manager of a Sears, Roebuck store.

b. The production manager of the upholstery installation department in an automobile manufacturing plant.

c. The sales manager of the Moody Company.

5. The owner of a chain of eight sporting goods stores in a large city says that the only control device he uses in measuring performance is net profits. What are the pros and cons of this approach? Would you recommend any additional controls? If so, which ones, and why?

NOTES

1. For instance, R. Alec McKenzie, *The Time Trap: Managing Your Way Out* (New York: American Management Association, 1972).

2. Lester R. Bittel, *Management by Exception* (New York: McGraw-Hill Book Co., 1964), p. 5.

Part 2

Operative Management

4

Motivation: Understanding the Why of Human Behavior

As we indicated in Chapter 1, a number of people believe management can never become a science because managers have to deal with human behavior, which is often unpredictable and irrational, and deal with human beings, who often act from emotion rather than reason. No social scientists would question that people often act emotionally; however, many would question that, except for the mentally ill, most of their behavior is irrational and unpredictable. They would insist that if more people understood the *why* of human behavior, it would seem less irrational and unpredictable. In the last two decades there has been much research on the behavior of people on the job, and some significant insights have been developed of vital importance to anyone in a position of leadership who wants to avoid unnecessary frictions and problems that can develop from his relationships with other people in the organization.

ABRAHAM MASLOW'S THEORY ON THE HIERARCHY OF NEEDS

Some students do not enjoy studying theory because they feel it is abstract and unrelated to the real world. Actually, whatever the discipline, good theory provides a basis for understanding, explaining, and predicting what will happen in the real world. The late social psychologist Kurt Lewin once said that nothing is more practical than good theory.[1] For a man of action, such as a manager who has to work with and through people, an understanding of motivation theory is essential.

In our opinion, the most significant and practical theory in the area of motivation has been developed by psychologist Abraham H. Maslow.[2] This particular theory is known as the *hierarchy of needs* concept, and its validity and practicality have been strengthened through various field-research studies of people in different organizations.[3] In fact, many social and behavioral scientists now accept this theory as the primary basis for explaining the behavior of people, both on and off the job.

Two principles provide the foundation of Maslow's theory: first, that human needs are arranged in a hierarchy or triangle of importance, and, second, that a satisfied need is not a primary motivator of behavior. To understand the significance of these two principles, let us examine the triangle of needs, as shown in Figure 12, and then elaborate on each level. The general idea is that as soon as a lower level in the triangle is relatively well satisfied, man attempts to satisfy needs at the next higher level. The problem is that many times he is blocked from need fulfillment at a higher level and this block will have behavioral consequences.

Figure 12. Maslow's hierarchy or triangle of human needs.

To illustrate, let us turn to the words of the late management theorist Douglas McGregor. More than anyone else, McGregor stated the theory in terms of an industrial setting and demonstrated the significance of the theory to management.

Physiological Needs

Man is a wanting animal—as soon as one of his needs is satisfied, another appears in its place. This process is unending. It continues from birth to death.

Man's needs are organized in a series of levels—a hierarchy of importance. At the lowest level, but preeminent in importance when they are thwarted, are his *physiological needs*. Man lives for bread alone, when there is no bread. Unless the circumstances are unusual, his needs for love, for status, for recognition are inoperative when his stomach has been empty for a while. But when he eats regularly and adequately, hunger ceases to be an important motivation. The same is true of the other physiological needs of man—for rest, exercise, shelter, protection from the elements.

A satisfied need is not a motivator of behavior! This is a fact of profound significance that is regularly ignored in the conventional approach to the management of people. Consider your own need for air: Except as you are deprived of it, it has no appreciable motivating effect upon your behavior.

Safety Needs

When the physiological needs are reasonably satisfied, needs at the next higher level begin to dominate man's behavior—to motivate him. These are called *safety needs*. They are needs for protection against danger, threat, deprivation. Some people mistakenly refer to these as needs for security. However, unless man is in a dependent relationship where he fears arbitrary deprivation, he does not demand security. The need is for the "fairest possible break." When he is confident of this, he is more than willing to take risks. But when he feels threatened or dependent, his greatest need is for guarantees, for protection, for security.

The fact needs little emphasis that, since every industrial employee is in a dependent relationship, safety needs may assume considerable importance. Arbitrary management

actions, behavior which arouses uncertainty with respect to
continued employment or which reflects favoritism or discrimination, unpredictable administration of policy—these
can be powerful motivators of the safety needs in the employment relationship *at every level*, from worker to vice president.

Social Needs

When man's physiological needs are satisfied and he is no
longer fearful about his physical welfare, his *social needs*
become important motivators of his behavior—needs for
belonging, for association, for acceptance by his fellows, for
giving and receiving friendship and love.

Management knows today of the existence of these needs,
but it often assumes quite wrongly that they represent a
threat to the organization. Many studies have demonstrated
that the tightly knit, cohesive work group may, under proper
conditions, be far more effective than an equal number of
separate individuals in achieving organizational goals.

Yet management, fearing group hostility to its own objectives, often goes to considerable lengths to control and
direct human efforts in ways that are inimical to the natural
"groupiness" of human beings. When man's social needs—are
perhaps his safety needs, too—are thus thwarted, he behaves
in ways which tend to defeat organizational objectives. He
becomes resistant, antagonistic, uncooperative. But this
behavior is a consequence, not a cause.

Ego Needs

Above the social needs—in the sense that they do not become motivators until lower needs are reasonably satisfied—
are the needs of greatest significance to management and to
man himself. They are the *egoistic needs*, and they are of two
kinds:

1. Those needs that relate to one's self-esteem—needs for
self-confidence, for independence, for achievement, for
competence, for knowledge.

2. Those needs that relate to one's reputation—needs for
status, for recognition, for appreciation, for the deserved
respect of one's fellows.

Unlike the lower needs, these are rarely satisfied; man

seeks indefinitely for more satisfaction of these needs once they have become important to him. But they do not appear in any significant way until physiological, safety, and social needs are all reasonably satisfied.

The typical industrial organization offers few opportunities for the satisfaction of these egoistic needs to people at lower levels in the hierarchy. The conventional methods of organizing work, particularly in mass-production industries, give little heed to these aspects of human motivation. If the practices of scientific management were deliberately calculated to thwart these needs, they could hardly accomplish this purpose better than they do.

Self-Fulfillment Needs

Finally—a capstone, as it were, on the hierarchy of man's needs—there are what we may call the *needs for self-fulfillment*. These are the needs for realizing one's own potentialities, for continued self-development, for being creative in the broadest sense of that term.

It is clear that the conditions of modern life give only limited opportunity for these relatively weak needs to obtain expression. The deprivation most people experience with respect to other lower-level needs divers their energies into the struggle to satisfy *those* needs, and the needs for self-fulfillment remain dormant.[4]

Making the Theory Come to Life: Two Examples

Several points need to be reemphasized; this can best be accomplished through two examples.

Example 1—The Manager Out of Work. Although the theory indicates that when the lower level needs are relatively well satisfied they cease to be important motivators of behavior, they can come back in a rush when threatened or taken away from a person. Take, for example, a middle-level manager working for an oil company in his hometown of Beaumont, Texas, a graduate of Texas A & M, and happily married. Although not wealthy, he is from an old and respected family, and his only daughter was recently honored by being selected as a debutante in Beaumont.

In twenty years with the oil company the manager has made steady advancement. His present salary is $24,000 a year. Perhaps more important, he has social standing and is a key member of an important company in a small city. Both in his work and in community activities he receives a great deal of satisfaction. In fact, he is operating in the need hierarchy at the highest levels. He rarely thinks of security or social needs because he takes them for granted.

Over a period of time two developments occur which change the manager's life. The first is a recession in the oil industry, which causes a great many men to be laid off work, including geologists and some staff men. The manager is shaken somewhat by this development, but he calculates that in his position and with his connections with the company he is safe. Unfortunately, a large corporation purchases the medium-sized company, and one of its first moves is to reduce the number of middle managers. Our friend is without a job.

What needs are important to this man now? Certainly they are not social needs, esteem, or self-fulfillment. Most important is security, because he realizes if he stays out of work long his entire world will collapse. His primary motivation now is to gain the security that can come only from finding another job.

Example 2—The Satisfied Work Force That Becomes Dissatisfied. The Maslow theory can be used to explain and predict not only individual but also group behavior, especially of people whose work is closely related and brings them into contact with one another. Consider, for example, a situation where a garment plant was built in a small Southern town in the early 1950s. This plant was the first to be located in the town and it provided needed employment for women whose husbands were eking out a living farming poor soil. The county in which the town was located was characterized by many small farms and had been losing population for over a decade.

For the first four years, the morale of the women working in the plant was quite high. In many families the women were bringing in more income than their husbands, and for the first time a number of the families were living above a subsistence level. Perhaps because of their gratitude to management, the women were not interested in a union and believed management to be quite fair in all matters.

Then, as a result of the efforts of the state's industrial-development group, a large, blue-chip national corporation decided to build another plant in the town. Among other things, the corporation was attracted by the large number of potential male employees residing in the county. Since the corporation's other plants were unionized, it encouraged the employees to affiliate with an international union and they did. Many of the men working for the new plant were husbands of the women working in the garment plant.

Six months after the new plant moved into town, the women employees voted in a union, despite an all-out campaign by management to prevent their doing so. It does not take much imagination to explain what happened or even to have predicted the event. In this case, the women talked with their husbands and discovered all sorts of things that they felt a need for in their own plant. For example, the men explained that, except for a few specific offenses such as stealing, a foreman could not arbitrarily fire a worker until the worker was given three warnings. Even then, workers had a grievance procedure whereby such a decision could be appealed. Moreover, in laying off workers in slack times, management was required to follow a lay-off system based on seniority. These things were unheard of in the garment plant. Although the women expected their husbands to receive a much higher hourly wage, they were quite upset that their husbands received three times as many paid holidays.

The moral of this story is that when people are operating at below or near subsistence they will be motivated to work for low wages and even be satisfied with poor working conditions. They may even be satisfied under such conditions for awhile; however, once they are made aware that there is more to life— once they feel reasonably well satisfied at the lowest level—they naturally want, expect, and demand more. The so-called carrot-and-stick approach does not work too well once a person moves beyond the subsistence level.

Qualifications to Maslow's Theory

The Maslow theory should be considered as a general guide to the leader who has to work with and through people. It is a relative concept, not an absolute explanation of all human behavior. Thus, there are four important qualifications one should be aware of:

First, one should not assume that each level in the triangle has to be satisfied 100 percent before the next need level emerges. Second, the theory does not pretend to explain the behavior of the neurotic or mentally disturbed. Third, there are other exceptions to the theory—for example, creative people who practically starve while trying to achieve self-actualization through creating a great work of art. Moreover, some people are much less security oriented or achievement oriented than others. Fourth, the theory states that a satisfied need is not a motivator of behavior, yet the two highest levels (unlike the lower levels) can hardly ever be fully satisfied: there are always new challenges and opportunities for growth, recognition, and achievement, and in the creative organization, a person may remain in the same job position for years and still find a great deal of challenge and motivations through his work.

HOW THE SUPERVISOR AFFECTS SUBORDINATES' LOWER LEVEL NEED SATISFACTION

The two higher level needs, McGregor points out, are the ones that people find blocked most often in the industrial setting. But the lower level needs are also vitally important. To show this, let us examine the role the supervisor plays in creating an environment to satisfy the lower level needs of the employees.

The Difficulty of Being a Leader

Being an effective leader is not easy, especially in the business world with its numerous and sometimes conflicting demands on a supervisor. To be an effective leader at any level, a person needs a wide range of knowledge and must be prepared to work hard throughout his career to broaden his knowledge and increase his insights. In short, being an effective leader requires hard work—work that does not stop with a few years' experience.

Actually, if more people knew how difficult it is to be successful as a leader, probably fewer would aspire to be leaders. In addition, although many people aspire to be leaders, quite a few are not successful because they do not have the intelligence, drive, perseverance, and ability to grow and develop. For those who become leaders, the demands are great. At the same time, the rewards and personal satisfaction are also great.

A successful leader is in a position not only to satisfy many of his own needs, wants, and aspirations, but also to act as the primary determinant of the satisfaction or the lack of satisfaction of the needs, wants, and aspirations of his subordinates. There is a so-called *law of effect*, which holds that those activities that meet with pleasurable consequences tend to be repeated, whereas those activities that meet with unpleasurable consequences tend not to be repeated. Since the supervisor in most companies has control of the reward and discipline system for his subordinates, he controls the reins of the law of effect. Through this influence, the immediate supervisor, more than any other person, is responsible for whether his employees develop into an excellent, fair, or poor work team.

What Subordinates Expect of Their Supervisor[5]

Although subordinates in a company are in a dependent position with respect to employment, pay increases, and the fulfillment of other needs and aspirations, this does not mean, of course, that a supervisor can manipulate them at will as he would a piece of equipment. The advent of unions, alternate employment opportunities, and more enlightened management practices have, we hope, ended forever this misguided notion of supervision. Employees now expect fair treatment by superiors, equitable wages, and decent conditions of employment. Sometimes industrial managers overlook this fact, and when they do, the business has difficulty achieving its objectives. To appreciate this fact, let us examine the expectations workers have of their immediate supervisor.

Knowledge. Most employees expect that the company will provide them with information on company policies, rules, and regulations, and that their supervisors will provide them with knowledge of their duties and responsibilities. Most companies and supervisors do a fair job in providing this type of information.

However, the employee has a right to expect more, and this is where many companies and supervisors fail. For example, new employees need to know what the probationary period is before they are accepted as full-fledged members of the organization, what assistance they can count on to help them become proficient in their work, on what basis they will receive promotions and pay increases, and how the company determines who will be first laid off in slack times. In addition, all employees need to be given advance notice on changes that may affect them. Finally and probably most important, employees need to get feedback on how they are performing. Employees not only need this knowledge, they expect it as part of their employment contract.

Atmosphere of Approval. Employees need to work in an atmosphere of approval, or an atmosphere free of fault finding. McGregor has pointed out that this atmosphere is independent of the superior's standards of performance and the strictness of his discipline. Rather this atmosphere depends more on the supervisor's attitudes toward his subordinates and how he corrects a subordinate who is doing something wrong—whether he uses the situation to help the subordinate do a better job in the future or to make him feel like an ignoramus who made a stupid mistake. By helping employees overcome learning mistakes in a positive manner, a supervisor is not being slack or easy. And certainly if a new employee simply cannot master the work during his probationary period, the supervisor should tell him so and let him know he should be transferred or dismissed.

Consistent Discipline. Most subordinates expect and want consistent discipline. One of the worst mistakes a supervisor can make is to try to be a nice guy and turn his back when subordinates violate company rules and policies. Invariably what happens is that sooner or later the supervisor has to crack down, and then his subordinates feel that he is playing favorites because he let other employees get by with rule breaking earlier. Discipline should be consistent not only in application to wrong actions but also in support of right actions. In other words, subordinates should have positive, supporting discipline when they do things beyond the normal expectations of their jobs. If you as a supervisor consciously keep on the lookout for ways to compliment your subordinates sincerely—to consistently give praise and acknowledgement to different people for similar types of achievements— you will be amazed at the esprit de corps this practice creates in your department.

HIGHER LEVEL NEEDS AND FREDERICK HERZBERG'S FINDINGS

Most of the actions of the supervisor discussed above relate to satisfaction of lower level needs, since the initial expectations of subordinates in their first jobs relate to their lower level needs, particularly the security need. But after an environment has been provided to satisfy employees' lower level needs, supervisors may try to tap the motivations to fulfill higher level needs. It is by tapping these needs that real achievements in efficiency, productivity, and creativity can take place in working with and through people.

Several recent motivation-research experiments have demonstrated the importance of higher level needs as motivators. The originator of these experiments is Frederick Herzberg, an American psychologist who has gained an international reputation in motivation and management theory. The findings have had considerable impact on American Management, and partly as a result of Herzberg's research, several leading American corporations have modified their programs of management and supervisory training and their organizational structure.

Herzberg's Original Study on Job Satisfaction

In the initial study, Herzberg and his associates conducted in-depth interviews with 200 engineers and accountants from eleven different firms in the Pittsburgh, Pennsylvania area.[6] Each person interviewed was asked to recall an event or incident or series of related events or incidents from the past year that made him feel unusually good about his work. He was also asked to speculate on how much the event or events affected his performance and morale. Conversely, he was asked to recall an event that made him feel unusually bad, and to speculate about its effect on performance and morale.

When Herzberg and his associates assessed the interviews, they found the top-ranking factors causing job satisfaction were achievement, recognition, work itself, responsibility, and advancement. The top-ranking factors causing job dissatisfaction were company policy and administration, supervision, relationship with supervisor, working conditions, and salary.

Most important, in almost all cases, the factors causing job satisfaction had a stimulating effect on performance and morale, whereas the factors causing job dissatisfaction had a negative effect. Another important finding was that the positive factors were all *intrinsic* to the job, whereas the negative factors were all *extrinsic*. That is, as management consultant Saul Gellerman pointed out: "When these men felt good about their jobs, it was usually because something had happened which showed that they were doing their work particularly well or that they were becoming more expert in their professions. Good feelings were, in other words, keyed to the specific tasks that the men performed, rather than to background factors such as money, security, or working conditions. On the other hand, when they felt bad it was usually because some disturbance in these background factors had caused them to believe that they were being treated unfairly."[7]

Herzberg and his associates therefore made a distinction between what they called motivators and hygienic factors. *Motivators* have uplifting effects on attitudes or performance. *Hygienic factors* prevent losses of morale or efficiency; although they cannot motivate by themselves, they can forestall any serious dissatisfaction or drop in productivity and allow the motivators to operate. As Gellerman observes, however, "the important point about hygienic factors is that they do nothing to elevate the individual's desire to do his job well."

The Herzberg study supports the validity of Maslow's concept of a hierarchy of needs—the "motivators" relate to the two highest levels (esteem and self-fulfillment) and the "hygenic factors" relate to the lower level needs, primarily the security needs.

What all this means is that people today expect to be treated fairly by their supervisors. They expect decent working conditions and pay comparable to that of people doing similar work in other firms. They expect company policies to be consistently and equitably applied to all employees. When these expectations are not realized, people are motivated in a negative sense, which usually is reflected in inefficiency and a high turnover rate. As the hierarchy of needs theory maintains, it is only when these lower levels are satisfied that the higher levels can be used most effectively in motivating people.

Additional Studies on Job Satisfaction

After the original Herzberg study with engineers and accountants, critics were quick to point out that while the findings might apply to professionals who sought creativity in their work, it would not apply to other groups of employees. But this criticism is not valid, for similar studies by different investigators in different countries have shown (except for minor deviations) surprisingly similar results. Figure 13 summarizes the results of twelve studies involving all manner of people: accountants, argicultural administrators, assemblers, engineers, food handlers, foremen, hospital main-tenance personnel, housekeepers, manufacturing supervisors, military officers, nurses, professional women, retired managers, scientists, teachers, and technicians.[8]

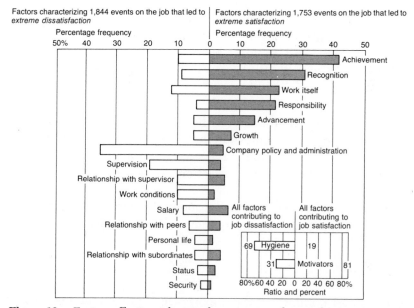

Figure 13. Factors affecting job attitudes, as reported in twelve investigations. (The percentage of satisfaction was based on a study of 1753 events on the job, the percentage of dissatisfaction was based on a study of 1844 events on the job.)

Although supervision is characterized as a hygienic factor, it should not be concluded that supervision is not important in positively motivating employees. In the summary of the twelve studies, ineffective supervision was ranked as the second most important factor in causing job dissatisfaction. One of the authors, in a study in New Zealand, discovered that ineffective supervision ranked as the number one factor in causing job dissatisfaction. A quote from a New Zealander illustrates how poor supervision can prevent positive motivation:

I was once given a job to do that involved a bit of responsibility. The job, I was told, was to take several days, and I was to be completely responsible for the job. I was told to report back at a later date and inform the boss how I was getting on. I didn't particularly worry when a couple of hours later the boss came down and asked me; in fact, I was quite glad that he was taking an interest. However, when he repeated the process at intervals of every two or three hours, I got decidedly annoyed. In fact, I was fed up, and I was looking for ways and means of palming the job off on to someone else. I felt that the boss thought I was incapable of doing the job properly, and I wondered why he gave it to me in the first place. The more I thought about this the more unhappy I got. Consequently, I began to take longer on the job than I should have done, and couldn't have cared less if it was right or wrong. After all, the boss was constantly checking it so he would pick up any mistakes.[9]

Thus, supervision is one of the major influences on whether such "motivators" as achievement, recognition, work itself, and responsibility are operating in the work environment—in short, on whether higher level need satisfaction can be realized by employees in their work.

In the next chapter we will examine how different leadership styles affect productivity and employee need satisfaction.

SUMMARY

This chapter pointed out the importance of understanding the *why* of motivation. We reviewed concepts from Maslow, McGregor, and Herzberg especially relevant to operative managers. In addition, we demonstrated that operative managers are, in effect, needs-controllers and have more to do with the satisfaction and development of employees than any other persons or factors within an organization.

QUESTIONS

1. Briefly outline Maslow's need hierarchy. What are the two basic principles underlying his theory? Can you relate the theory to a real situation?

2. What kinds of knowledge should the leader furnish his subordinates? How does this information satisfy their needs?
3. What findings resulted from Frederick Herzberg's research concerning employee motivation? Can these findings be correlated with Maslow's need hierarchy?
4. Do you now believe that an employee is best motivated by "paying him more money" or by "punishing him if he does not perform satisfactorily"?
5. Is security the most important job need of blue-collar workers?

NOTES

1. Quoted in Alfred J. Marrow, *Behind the Executive Mask* (New York: American Management Association, 1965), p. 7.
2. Abraham H. Maslow, *Motivation and Personality* (New York: Harper & Row 1954).
3. Probably the most significant has been Lyman W. Porter's study, "Organizational Patterns of Managerial Job Attitudes," sponsored by the American Foundation for Management Research.
4. Douglas M. McGregor, "The Human Side of Enterprise," *Management Review* November, 1957, pp. 22–28. Reprinted by permission of the publisher, © 1957 by the American Management Association, Inc.
5. The material in this section is adapted from Douglas McGregor's article "Conditions of Effective Leadership in the Industrial Organization," which first appeared in the *Journal of Consulting Psychology*, March-April, 1944, pp. 55–63.
6. Frederick Herzberg, Bernard Mausner, and Barbara Snyderman, *The Motivation to Work* (New York: John Wiley & Sons, 1959).
7. Saul Gellerman, *Motivation and Productivity* (New York: American Management Association, 1963), p. 49.
8. Frederick Herzberg, "One More Time: How Do You Motivate Employees?", *Harvard Business Review*, January-February, 1968, pp. 53–62.
9. Donald Mosley, "What Motivates New Zealanders?" *Management* (official journal of the New Zealand Institute of Management), October, 1969, p. 37.

5

Supervision: Six Styles of Leadership

No topic is of greater interest than styles of leadership. In conducting management development programs, we find that practicing managers are keenly interested in this subject. Why do some leaders use one style and other leaders use another? What effects do different styles have on employees' productivity and morale? What style is most appropriate in a particular situation? Should a particular style be used consistently or changed as circumstances seem to change? Such questions are vital for an organization, since supervisory behavior is one of the primary determinants of organizational performance and productivity.

THE CHOICE OF A LEADERSHIP STYLE

Whether they are consciously aware of it or not, most people in leadership positions rely on a predominant supervisory style in working with and through people. This style is affected by several factors. Three of the important ones are, first, a person's family and early school environment while he was growing up; second, his past experience and training in the area of leadership; and third, his present work environment (including type of work engaged in, his superior's leadership style, and the general management system).

These factors interact to influence his view of the nature of man and consequently his management philosophy. For example, consider how a person was treated in his early home environment. Was he given encouragement, praise, approval? Was he treated fairly and provided with consistent discipline? All these can significantly affect his choice of leadership style later on. Past experience and training in leadership is also a factor. If the two past leaders a person most admired were his high school football coach and his army company commander, both stern disciplinarians who nonetheless achieved effective results, it is quite possible the young man placed in a supervisory position with a business firm will pattern his leadership style after these two men. Finally, a person's present work environment may affect his choice of a leadership style. If a supervisor works for a firm where most of the decisions ae made by top management and the initiation of ideas from lower levels is discouraged, this environment could discourage the supervisor from adopting a participative style of leadership, even though he might prefer it.

Unfortunately, many people use a less effective style than they could be using, often because they do not realize the benefits of other styles. Moreover, the most effective style in one situation may not be the most effective in another. Let us therefore examine six different styles—their characteristics, their relationship to the hierarchy of needs, their impact on people, and when they can be used most effectively. The styles overlap somewhat and not every leader will use one particular style but may draw from several different ones in working with and through people. The six styles appear as follows as if placed on a spectrum: *autocratic, close, general, participative, democratic,* and *permissive* (see Figure 14).

AUTOCRATIC SUPERVISION

Autocratic leadership may also be called the authoritarian or "be strong" approach. The autocratic leader generally does not trust people. He believes that many will try to get away with doing as little as possible, and so he makes use of extensive close controls and checks to ensure that his subordinates perform as expected.

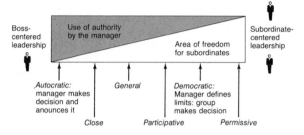

Figure 14. Continuum of leadership behavior. (Adapted from Robert H. Tannenbaum and Warren H. Schmidt, "How to Choose a Leadership Pattern," *Harvard Business Review*, March-April, 1958, p. 98. Footnote omitted.)

The autocrat also relies on the use of power or the threat of it to get things done. For example, he uses fear and threats of punitive action if subordinates do not measure up. One of the authors recalls an autocratic leader saying "I don't give a damn whether my men like me or not, just so long as they do what I ask and show me respect." As might be expected, the autocratic leader is usually a strict disciplinarian and, if he has the authority to do so, does not mind firing people if they do not perform as he expects.

In communicating with subordinates he relies primarily on instructions and orders. His philosophy and manner provide little opportunity for subordinates to question his instructions or participate in decision making. He rarely relies on group meetings except, like a military commander, to pass along instructions. To him, people are expendable—results are what count—and so he chooses people in his own image, that is, who subscribe to his way of operating. Sometimes, when the work load has increased to the point where the leader is in danger of losing control, he will delegate more authority to a subordinate than he would under normal circumstances.

Impact on People and Relationship to the Hierarchy of Needs

The effects of the "be strong" approach on people have been criticized as follows:[1]

1. This policy normally provides no incentive to work harder than the minimum required to avoid punishment. . . .

2. The essence of "be strong" is the application of pressure. But when subjected to too much pressure employees fight back. When they can they fight through their union. Even if they have no union, they engage in slowdowns, sabotage, and spoilage. . . .

3. To protect themselves from pressure employees, organize groups and cliques . . . and already-existing groups may be drawn closer together and take on a new purpose, that of protecting themselves against management pressure.

4. Probably the most serious trouble with "be strong" is that it ignores a basic factor in human behavior. When people are put under too much pressure they become frustrated . . . when people become frustrated they react in strange ways that tend to reduce the effectiveness of the organization in its main task of getting out production.

One of the most serious deficiencies of the authoritarian approach is that it provides little opportunity for employees to grow and develop on the job, since, after all, the boss makes all the decisions. An authoritarian leader may be effective in achieving satisfactory results, but often when he leaves, his department begins to produce unsatisfactory results, unless he is replaced by an unusually competent leader.

In the hierarchy of needs, subordinates rarely move beyond the lower levels in this work environment. This explains why a high turnover rate within a department can many times be traced to an autocratic leader. The only person who receives higher level need satisfaction is the leader himself. Certainly some leaders receive satisfaction from the power that comes from making all the decisions and using the "be strong" approach.

When Autocratic Supervision Is and Is Not Effective

Although autocracy is one of the predominant leadership styles, there are few American industries and situations where this approach would prove most effective over the long run. Certainly this conclusion would be true for professional and skilled workers. Some people have argued that the authoritarian approach is most effective with unskilled or seasonal workers; however, this is not the case, although it might be during an economic recession.

The authoritarian approach appears to be most successful when it is used as a temporary strategy for a particular situation rather than as the predominant style of the leader. For example, consider a leader whose predominant style is more participative in working with and through people. Most of the people respond well in this environment, but let us assume two employees are continually late with their work and frequently make excuses and blame others for their ineffectiveness. Perhaps the best way to motivate them is for the leader to use a "be strong" approach, with the ultimate threat of dismissal if they do not improve their effectiveness.

One of the authors observed a large bottling company, whose managers used a participative leadership approach, acquire a failing medium-sized company with a weak management that used a permissive type of leadership. Although it was not its basic philosophy, the larger company adopted a very autocratic approach the first year in dealing with its new subsidiary. It fired some people, dictated operating procedures and policies, and maintained close control to see that these instructions were followed. This "be strong" approach worked and made an unprofitable operation profitable, and so the parent organization gradually reduced the pressure and changed to a more participative approach.

Of course, there *are* some successful autocratic leaders—for example, the late Vince Lombardi, the successful and colorful coach of the Green Bay Packers and Washington Redskins. Lombardi was noted for his hard-nosed approach to the game of football, and he used fear as a motivating force with many players.

CLOSE SUPERVISION

Close supervision is somewhat similar to the autocratic approach, but it has several major differences, the most important, perhaps, being that it does not emphasize firing a person if he does not move in the right direction. In fact, a number of people who practice close supervision are mild mannered, yet possess one characteristic of the autocrat: they do not trust people. They believe in close control and close supervision, many times doing the same type of work as the men they are supervising.

Close supervision is practiced by a large number of supervisors in American industry, a fact pinpointed by a University of Michigan survey of leadership in different business organizations. It discovered that close supervision reflects the following characteristics:

1. The close supervisor spends 50 percent or more of his time doing the same type of work as the senior people in his section.
2. The close supervisor delegates much less than the participative supervisor and tends to give frequent and detailed instructions and in general limits the freedom of subordinates to do the work in their own way.
3. The close supervisor spends much less time than the general supervisor in trying to secure promotions and pay increases for his men.
4. The close supervisor when asked the most important part of his job invariably stresses the production and technical aspects—in other words to get production out with a given amount of equipment, materials, and men.[2]

This last characteristic is illustrated by the statement of a manager who practices close supervision that "This interest in people is all right, but it is a luxury. I've got to keep pressure on production, and when I get production up, then I can afford to take time to show an interest in my employees and their problems."

Impact on People and Relationship to the Hierarchy of Needs

Achievement-oriented employees find it quite frustrating and demoralizing to work under close supervision, especially for prolonged periods. Consequently, departments where close supervision is practiced tend to have high turnover in personnel. We need only relate the characteristics of close supervision to the hierarchy of needs to see why this is true. There is little opportunity for subordinates to satisfy higher level needs when the supervisor is working with them constantly and giving them detailed and frequent instructions on what to do.

When Close Supervision Is and Is Not Effective

The University of Michigan research indicates that most close supervisors are in charge of departments that are low in productivity—a highly ironic fact, since most such supervisors are company oriented and want to achieve high production. In essence, the very zeal to meet company expectations may cause a number of supervisors to resort to close supervision. They feel that in this manner they may stay on top of things and ensure that company goals are met.

To illustrate this point, let us cite the experience of a maintenance department in a medium-sized plant which had an excessively high turnover and was not achieving the maintenance results that management expected. One of the authors was called in as consultant and discovered that the pay, fringe benefits, and so on, were the highest in the area. Thus, it was hypothesized that the problem might involve supervision. Accordingly, in-depth interviews were conducted with maintenance employees, maintenance supervisors, and the department head in order to determine the various leadership styles used by the foremen.

The results indicated that three of the supervisors were highly respected workers, spent considerable time training and developing appprentices, used senior mechanics in training and in helping with maintenance problems, and in general used a participative style of leadership. The other five supervisors, however, used either autocratic or close supervision in overseeing the men. The problem was compounded because every three months the different teams of maintenance workers were rotated to a new supervisor. Further investigation revealed that the autocratic and close supervisors were the least effective in achieving results.

Prior to this investigation, top management had assumed incorrectly that the most effective foreman was one who practiced close supervision. This particular foreman was a man of high intelligence, was previously an excellent mechanic, and was very loyal to the company—so loyal, in fact, that often he would require his crew to work through lunch hour in order to finish a maintenance assignment. He supervised so closely that he would even tell his men how to perform the simplest task. When interviewed one mechanic complained about how upsetting it was to work under a participative foreman who gave him freedom to do the work his own way, then be assigned to the close-supervising foreman who specified exactly how to do the job. Thus, the mechanic added, the crew made a game of finding subtle ways to slow down the work and make the foreman look foolish.

Close supervision, then, is not very effective when the work requires any type of initiative or creativity in subordinates. However, it might work well with new employees, employees with low IQs, or in the short run in a department where costs have become excessive or where an emergency job must be accomplished.

We will now turn from the autocratic and close supervision styles to other styles. However, we shall examine only the characteristics of each style, leaving it to you to draw from your own experience and explore the impact of these styles on people, their relationship to the hierarchy of needs, and when they might be effective or ineffective.

GENERAL SUPERVISION

The University of Michigan researchers discovered that general supervision is also widely used in American industry. When asked the most important feature of their jobs, leaders practicing general supervision stressed human relations and the development of subordinates—thus impelling the researchers to characterize the general supervisor as "employee centered." This does not mean the general supervisor ignored the production or task requirements of his department, rather that he emphasized working with and through people in such a way that effective results would naturally follow.

The published research and the authors' own experience in identifying leadership styles suggest that there are four main characteristics of a general supervisor. First, he delegates authority and supervises by results. Although he sets definite assignments, standards, and goals, he usually provides only general instructions and guidelines, leaving the "how" part and specific details to his subordinates.

Second, he emphasizes training and developing of subordinates, through the process of delegation of authority and supervision by results. When the results are standard or above, he gives recognition by providing a positive feedback. When the results are below standard, he uses a counseling session to try to discover why the results are not as they should be and how improvement can be achieved. Consciously or unconsciously, the general supervisor seems to realize that for learning and development to be effective, there must be an active process with the employees involved. In addition, he is confident that people will learn from their own mistakes if corrective feedback takes place in a positive environment.

Third, the general supervisor spends half or more of his time planning and organizing the work of his department and coordinating with other departments and supervisors. Primarily because of delegation, he has more time to engage in these important activities than does the leader who practices close supervision.

Fourth and finally, the general supervisor is more accessible to talk over departmental or personal problems of subordinates than is the close supervisor. Perhaps because of his emphasis on people as human resources, he also spends more time in trying to win deserving employees pay increases and promotions.

PARTICIPATIVE SUPERVISION

The participative style of leadership goes a step beyond general supervision in involving employees. Whereas a general supervisor himself sets the standards, objectives, and goals of his department and the individuals in it, the participative supervisor invites departmental members to share with him the setting of such standards and the like.

To illustrate how a leader might encourage this type of participation, let us examine briefly the steps of joint target-setting or management by objectives. First the individual discusses his job description with his superior and they agree on the content of his job and the relative importance of his major duties—the things he is paid to do and is accountable for. Next the subordinate establishes performance targets for each of his responsibilities for the forthcoming period and meets with his superior to discuss his target program. Checkpoints are then established to evaluate his progress, and ways of measuring progress are selected. Finally, superior and subordinate meet at the end of the period to discuss the results of the subordinate's efforts to meet the targets he established.[4] In this process, the supervisor shares with his subordinate the setting of his targets and goals, but he reserves veto power and final decision-making authority.

DEMOCRATIC SUPERVISION

Democratic is the ultimate in involving employees in the operation of a department and the sharing of decision making. But democratic differs from participative in that it uses more group involvement in goal setting and decision making. Moreover, the democratic leader does not reserve final decision-making authority; rather, he tries to create an environment so that consensus decision making will prevail. If this fails, he will commit the group to the majority viewpoint even if he holds a minority viewpoint.

The democratic leader maintains that human cooperation is a stronger force than competition, that group interaction provides a freer, more honest circulation of views and information, thus leading to more effective decisions and control. This leader also believes that high-performance goals can be established and that because of the group process individuals within the group will be more committed to the achievement of the goals.

PERMISSIVE SUPERVISION

The leader using a permissive style may or may not make use of group decision making. If he does, he may delegate completely the process to departmental members without participating himself.

One major characteristic of the permissive leader is that he is almost completely employee centered. Thus, he places an unusual amount of emphasis on interpersonal relations and on making concessions to employee requests. Some people call this "country-club leadership," since the primary emphasis is on keeping people happy.

Perhaps because he is so employee centered, the permissive supervisor slights or ignores the task side or the achievement of effective results. If effective results do occur, they are probably more or less accidental; they occur probably because two or three people within the department grab the ball and run with it. This leader is like the elementary-school teacher who places all the emphasis on social and group relationships, keeping the children happy with fun and games while ignoring the task side of learning mathematics, science, and English. In this environment, if some of the children do learn , it is probably because of their own efforts.

There is a difference between the permissive leader anxious to avoid disagreements at all costs and the democratic leader who encourages differences and provides opportunity for resolving and learning from them through the group process. Usually the democratic leader also places greater emphasis on the achievement of high performance goals.

INFLUENCE OF DOUGLAS McGREGOR'S MANAGEMENT PHILOSOPHIES ON LEADERSHIP STYLES

Just as certain background factors may influence an individual's view of the nature of man and thus his preferred leadership style, so may some management philosophies. There are several such philosophies (such as benevolent autocracy[4]), but two of the most widely publicized in industry today are Douglas McGregor's Theory X and Theory Y assumptions about the nature of man. McGregor summarizes these two contrasting sets of assumptions as follows.

The Assumptions of Theory X

1. The average human being has an inherent dislike of work and will avoid it if he can.
2. Because of this human characteristic—dislike of work— most people must be coerced, controlled, directed, threatened with punishment to get them to put forth adequate effort toward the achievement of organizational objectives.
3. The average human being prefers to be directed, wishes to avoid responsibility, has relatively little ambition, wants security above all.

The Assumptions of Theory Y

1. The expenditure of physical and mental effort in work is as natural as play or rest.
2. External control and the threat of punishment are not the only means for bringing about effort toward organizational objectives. Man will exercise self-direction and self-control in the service of objectives to which he is committed.

3. Commitment to objectives is a function of the rewards associated with their achievement.
4. The average human being learns, under proper conditions, not only to accept but to seek responsibility.
5. The capacity to exercise a relatively high degree of imagination, ingenuity, and creativity in the solution of organizational problems is widely, not narrowly, distributed in the population.
6. Under the conditions of modern industrial life the intellectual potentialities of the average human being are only partially utilized.[5]

You can readily see that a person holding theory X assumptions would prefer an autocratic style, whereas the person holding theory Y assumptions would prefer a more participative leadership style. Actually, the person holding theory Y assumptions would not always use a participative approach; although he might prefer it, the situation might call for another approach. For example, with new employees he might prefer to use close supervision and gradually evolve to a more participative style as the employees become more skilled and competent. As McGregor put it, in the use of participative management, sometimes employees have to learn to crawl and then walk before they learn to run.

The trend in American industry is for leaders, where feasible, to use more participative styles, sharing at least some power with subordinates. An explanation is that employees are becoming better educated and in many companies have their lower level needs relatively well satisfied; it is only through tapping the higher level needs, then, that significant motivation will occur. Finally, the evidence suggests that a leader should be concerned with both task requirements and employee needs, and that these two requirements need not be in opposition to one another.

SUMMARY

This chapter highlighted the characteristics of different leadership styles. The use of autocratic and close supervision reflects a lack of trust in subordinates and relies on frequent controls and checks. The primary difference between the two is that autocratic supervision relies more on power and the use of fear. General supervision delegates authority, sets definite standards, and supervises by results; in addition, considerable time is spent in planning and organizing the work and in counseling with subordinates. Both participative and democratic supervision use even more of a shared approach in developing people and making decisions regarding standards and goals of the department. Unfortunately, some people who attempt democratic supervision slip over into permissive leadership, which tends to slight or ignore the task side of work.

QUESTIONS

1. Briefly discuss the major factors that may influence the choice of an individual's leadership style. Correlate these factors with different leadership styles.
2. Do you believe the autocratic leader obtains the best results? In the short run? In the long run? Give some example situations where the autocrat would be effective.
3. What one characteristic do both the autocrat and the close supervisor possess?
4. Relate satisfaction of the individual needs (hierarchy) to performance under the different types of leaders.
5. In what way does the permissive leader compromise the task to be accomplished? Do you think his approach instills or allows a greater degree of individual initiative than other leadership styles?
6. Correlate McGregor's Theory X-Y to the spectrum of leadership styles.
7. Assume you have been recently hired as plant manager of Comapny Y to replace a capable plant manager who recently died. The old plant manager was a dynamic individual whose leadership was of the authoritarian type and who advocated close supervision. This leadership philosophy and approach has infiltrated and imbued all levels of management. You personally believe in the merits of general supervision. How would you handle this conflict? Include in your answer factors you would take into consideration and what action you would take if any.

NOTES

1. George Strauss and Leonard R. Sayles, *Personnel: The Human Problems of Management* (Englewood Cliffs, N.J.: Prentice-Hall, 1960), pp. 108–109.
2. See Rensis Likert, *New Patterns of Management* (New York: McGraw-Hill Book Company, 1961), p. 7.
3. Alva F. Kendall and James Gatza, "Positive Program for Performance Appraisal," *Harvard Business Review*, November-December, 1963, p. 155.
4. For an insight into this philosophy see Robert N. McMurray, "The Case for Benevolent Autocracy," *Harvard Business Review*, January-February, 1958, pp. 86–90.
5. Douglas McGregor, *The Human Side of Enterprise* (New York: McGraw-Hill Book Company, 1960), pp. 33–48.

6

The Informal Organization: Management's Unofficial Counterpart

When John Moody's boat-trailer company grew to reach its final stage, as we saw in Chapter 2, it achieved a structure that we were able to represent in a formal organization chart. This formal structure is based on officially established relationships recognized by management; the basis for these relationships is authority and responsibility. The typical organization chart may contain such things as a person's title, perhaps even a brief job description of duties and responsibilities. But it is lifeless. When we plug actual people into these positions, their likes, dislikes, backgrounds, personalities, and needs, then the informal organization begins to emerge.

Let us look behind the scenes—inside the offices and on the work floor. We will probably find that the important relationships in getting work accomplished are very different from those shown on the formal chart.

Let us assume that of his three second-level managers (finance, production, and sales) Moody holds the production manager in highest esteem—either because he has known him longest, believes him to be the most capable second-level manager, or feels he has given him excellent counsel and advice in the past. The sales and finance managers recognize their production colleague's influence with Moody and so frequently seek his assistance on matters they want to bring to Moody's attention and get his support on. Yet the formal chart shows that the three second-level managers have equal influence.

Likewise, on lower work levels, we may find some production foremen more effective and "in the know" than other foremen because of a closer relationship with their production department head. Even at the bottom level, some workers may be more respected by fellow workers because of their seniority or expertise or because certain jobs in the plant carry more status than others. We have seen many cases where workers on the same level consult with one particular fellow worker about job-related problems rather than with their supervisor. The types of relationships we are mentioning here are *not* shown on a formal organization chart. Yet they are an important fact of life in every organization.

Frequently, the "pecking order" of the informal organization is completely out of line with the formal organization chart that hangs in top management's office. We feel that in such cases the informal organization carries greater weight, since it describes the way things actually get done in an organization. We might say that the formal organization structure represents a type of "game plan" that management has set up in order to reach the organization's objectives. But just as many game plans are never put into practice, so many formal organization charts only remotely describe the important relationships that exist.

In this chapter, we will look at some reasons for and characteristics of informal organizations, for it is critical that a manager understand the nature of informal organization. The impression is frequently given that informal organization causes inefficiency. Although this can certainly be true, it just as frequently can cause greater efficiency, depending on the manager's ability to utilize it.

WHY INFORMAL GROUPS ARE FORMED

Man is a social animal. That is, he has basic social needs, as we pointed out earlier in examining Maslow's hierarchy of needs concept. A worker enjoys the companionship of his fellow workers on the job, the discussions that take place at breaks, the members who ride with him in the car pool, and the other players on the company bowling team. In fact, so important is this inclusion as "one of the boys" that the average worker is very careful not to do things that might cause him to lose favor with other group members.

But in addition to serving a worker's social need, the informal group also helps satisfy a worker's security need. The old "strength in numbers" axiom gives a worker a feeling of security in that his informal group will help resist what it considers unfair management practices. For example, management may pressure for higher output which workers feel is not justified. The informal group may react by setting a "bogey"—a specified amount of work that group members should not exceed. An individual worker, of course, would not be able to succeed at this mission by himself, but when an entire department engages in such restricted output, it can be highly effective in having management reconsider the higher work standards.

In another example, on the first days on a job, a new worker is bound to feel a certain amount of insecurity about the type of behavior expected of him. By joining groups on the job he can find out the "right thing to do" (how long to take for a coffee break, when to get a drink of water); the informal group will help satisfy his security need by pointing out the behavior expected of him and help him feel accepted by other members of the group.

FIRST RESEARCH ON INFORMAL GROUPS: THE HAWTHORNE STUDIES

The first real recognition that informal bonds existed among workers occurred in the late 1920s.[1] The "Hawthorne studies," conducted at the Hawthorne Plant of the Western Electric Company in Chicago, sought originally to see what impact changes in working conditions had on worker productivity. Among the changes tried in some work groups were rest breaks and snacks for workers and reduced working hours. During all of these experiments, worker productivity increased. However, when the experimental groups returned to the original work conditions (no breaks, full work day) worker productivity still continued at a high pace. The researchers were stumped.

Actually, what caused the workers to be more efficient was that they had become molded into a strong, informal team. They felt important in being singled out for the experiment and while it was going on they became closely knit. When one worker did not feel able to work well on a given day, his fellow workers took up the slack. The group not only became tightly knit; more important, it accepted the overall goal of increased productivity as its objective.

The Hawthorne researchers were fascinated to discover the important role informal groups actually played throughout the company. Various groups had their own informal leaders, their own recognized status systems, communications, and work standards, their own norms of behavior. Workers who exceeded the work standards paid a penalty—they were excluded from the group, ignored, even threatened with physical harm.

Thus, while the formal organization chart showed how things were supposed to work, who was supposed to have influence, who was supposed to enforce rules, regulations, and standards, the informal group actually determined many of these things. As a scholar pointed out about one such group,—"the internal function of this organization was to control and regulate the behavior of its members. Externally, however, it functioned as a protective mechanism. It served to protect the group from outside interference by manifesting a strong resistance to change, or threat of change in conditions of work and personal relations. . . . Had it been explicitly stated their behavior could be said to have been guided by the following rule: 'Let us behave in such a way as to give management the least opportunity of interfering with us.'"[2]

FIVE CHARACTERISTICS OF INFORMAL ORGANIZATIONS

We will discuss five characteristics of informal organizations: leadership, status, standards and norms, discipline, and communications.

Leadership

In the formal organization, authority and responsibility act as the process that bind and unite the organization's members; the president, vice-presidents, managers, supervisors, department heads, and foremen, because of their rank, hold the positions of appointed authority. The informal organization has no formal authority as such, although in practice there is something very close to it.

Consider the example of John Mason, a physically large man (6'4" and 230 pounds) and once a star athlete, who has been with the Leland Manufacturing Company for twelve years. John has trained many of the younger men in the maintenance department, and the men respect him for his ability and look up to him. Recently, management ruled that maintenance workers would have to wear a standard gray uniform for "appearance." During the lunch break, John tells the men in the maintenance department that he'll quit the company rather than wear this "army uniform." All the men in the department pledge to go along with him and they all sign a petition stating that if they have to wear a uniform, they will walk off the job. John Mason agrees to serve as spokesman for the group, just as he has on so many other occasions.

Thus, though John Mason has no formal authority over his fellow workers, his rank as their informal leader actually works very much the same. People go along with what he says, and so he is exercising an influence with the group that we can call leadership.

The informal group leader helps guide, direct, and steer his group's behavior. Indeed, there may be more than one leader in an informal group. For instance, one Hawthorne researcher noticed that two workers held rather privileged positions in their group and were looked up to by the rest of the members:

> On these two the group seemed to place considerable responsibility. Of "A" they said: "He can handle the engineers, inspectors, and the supervisors. They have to come to him if they want to know anything." In speaking of "B" they expressed admiration for his work habits and capacities. The common remarks about him were: "He taught me my job," "When he adjusts a machine, he never raises his eyes until it works," "So-and-so talked too much a while ago, and 'B' shut him up." Quite frequently "B" shows them an easy way to make an adjustment that is difficult because of a variation in the piece parts. All expressed appreciation of his willingness to help them.[3]

It is important that a manager recognize the informal leaders among workers in his department. Later we will show how an informal leader can be used to help accomplish management's formal objectives.

Status

The formal organization structure might lead you to believe that status follows closely the chain of command, but this is not necessarily so. In many companies, for example, white-collar office workers have higher status than shopworkers who receive higher pay. Or in other plants, a high-seniority worker in a skilled job has more informal status than a supervisor in an adjacent department where unskilled work is done. Thus, the type of work has much influence on the "respect" accorded by informal group members: the saleswoman in Fine Furs has more status than the saleswoman in Candy & Nuts; the auto salesman has more status than the mechanic. In manufacturing plants, the higher status jobs are usually cleaner and require less manual labor than lower status jobs.

In addition to the type of work done, other factors also influence one's status or the respect accorded by the informal organization: his title, pay, freedom from close supervision, work location, symbols such as office furnishings, or preferred parking space, and having an assistant or secretary.

A person's higher status in the informal group may be recognized in various ways. Other group members may ask for his views about job-related matters, especially if his higher status is accorded because of his expertise. Higher status may also dictate who takes coffee breaks where, when, and with whom, who cleans up first at the end of the day, and so on.

Standards and Norms

The formal organization obviously establishes certain standards and norms of behavior to help in reaching its objectives. For example, rules and policies help guide the behavior of organizational members in certain directions. A sales department may have formally established rules regarding dress of its sales representatives; it may have certain standards as to the minimum number of calls to be made per week, the forms to be used to record a sale, and so on. The operator of a drill press in a large manufacturing firm has standards as to the number and quality of operations to be conducted in a day. He is expected to follow the rules on working hours, rest breaks, and safety standards. Such formal standards and norms set by those in authority are a necessity in guiding an organization.

But the informal organization also imposes standards and norms of behavior on its members. The most common standard is the "bogey" or amount of work that group members should not exceed. This form of restricted output serves as a type of group protection, for if some workers consistently outperform others, it is feared that it will make the "average" performers look bad and perhaps cause management to raise its standard. The result is frequently an informal agreement that nobody should go all out. A work limit is informally set and workers understand that their work is to fall within the limits acceptable to the group. Thus, it is common to find that many above-average workers work at a fast pace early in the day and coast later in the day.

Perhaps you are thinking that informal groups tend to *restrict* output. This is not necessarily the case. Such standards can work both ways. We have seen cases where work groups set standards higher than management wanted and where informal group pride created workmanship of higher caliber than management classified acceptable. Groups themselves tend to have little regard for the goof-off, and put immense pressure on a low producer to feel that he is sharing the group's work load. The group's norms of behavior may also be helpful to management's objectives in other ways. For instance, some informal leaders on a football team may work out on their own after formal practice to prepare for an important game. The spirit becomes contagious and soon the entire team stays on for this extra preparation—to the point where the nonconformer risks his informal group membership. In another instance, the production worker who takes an extended smoke break may feel pressure from the group that, because of him, management may reduce or eliminate the break. Such group pressure has helped enforce many rules established by the formal organization.

Recently, one of the authors observed a training program for fifteen first-line manufacturing supervisors. In the early stages of the classes, one supervisor carried on in a rather childish manner, talking loudly to those next to him and joking and laughing. Evidently, he was not much interested in the program. While another supervisor was making a comment to the entire group, this particular supervisor began talking loudly to the man on his right. The supervisor who had the floor, obviously distracted, turned and said: "Bill, dammit, either quit acting like a child or get the hell out of here so we can learn something. We all know that you're too good to need any training." Bill apparently noted from the expressions on the faces of his fellow supervisors that his line of behavior had fallen out of line with the group's expectations, and so throughout the rest of the training sessions paid attention and participated as well as any of the other men.

Discipline

A parent, teacher, or coach uses discipline as a corrective measure in keeping behavior within prescribed limits. The formal organization keeps discipline by the formal authority vested in superiors, who may use oral discussions, written warnings, demotions, lay-offs, and ultimately firing. But the informal organization imposes a different type of discipline for behavior that falls out of line with the informal standards and norms.

Consider the case of Jules Hellman, one of several college students hired for the summer to work as a parts picker in an automobile parts warehouse. Jules, however was the son of the warehouse manager, and his attitude from the outset seemed to be one of superiority. He did not associate with the other men while on the job, and he took his breaks and ate lunch with the white-collar office workers rather than with the other men. He also consistently outperformed the other parts pickers by completing more orders than they did, and refused to abide by the pickers' informal privilege of washing up fifteen minutes before quitting time, working instead right up to the 5 P.M. bell. One day, an older worker casually mentioned to Jules that he was making some of the other men look bad with his rapid work pace, and suggested that Jules take his time and do the average day's work he was being paid for. Jules took offense, and promptly that day completed more orders than he had ever done before.

Then things began to happen. First, the supervisor warned him that some of the men had complained that he was pushing his four-wheel parts truck at a reckless pace, making the plant unsafe. The following day, he received twelve error slips from the packing department, either for having picked an incomplete order or for having some parts included that were not on the order. That afternoon, his truck, loaded with automobile fenders, lost a wheel, fell over, and damaged several fenders.

What accounted for these events? Whenever Jules left his truck unguarded, another worker would put on an unordered part or remove parts that Jules had properly picked. This accounted for the error slips Jules received. As for the truck losing a wheel, the cotter pin that held the wheel in place was never found.

That afternoon Jules took his break in the plant with the rest of the men, though sitting by himself. He also washed up at 4:45 P.M. like everybody else. In this incident, we find that Jules was paying a price for his violation of the group's norms and standards. Ostracism, or explusion from the group, is perhaps the most common measure taken against a person who fails to go along with group practices. For most of us, such a threat is a strong incentive to keep our behavior on a level that is acceptable to our fellow workers. For some individuals, however, group acceptance or membership is not as important as other considerations. Some feel a strong moral commitment to doing their best on a job, others are attracted by greater monetary rewards. The *rate buster*, as such people are called, is often a highly devout, religious, independent person who feels a greater need to produce high results on the job than to be one of the boys.

Many managers are perplexed at the failure of incentive systems to increase output. As one manager put it to one of the authors, "I don't know what's gone wrong. Our industrial engineers came up with a good piecework incentive system, but it hasn't caught on at all. I know these people could do better on the job, and bring in an extra ten or fifteen dollars a week without much extra effort. But the new piecework system hasn't done a bit of good, because everybody still does the same amount of work they did before the incentive went in." The answer to such a failure can often be traced to the workings of the informal organization, to the uncertainty that if workers' productivity rises, and they earn extra pay, management will then lower the piecework rate.

To these workers, group acceptance and satisfaction of the social need is more important than the additional money that could be earned by ignoring the group's bogey. As one worker confided, "No, we haven't had any problems with rate busters in our department. Sometimes we get a new guy who's pretty good, or just plain gung-ho, but he'll come around. Now I'm not saying everybody does the same amount of work, because we've got a few people who do more than the average. But they know when to start taking it easy. If we all produce at a good, easy pace, nobody comes out looking bad, and we don't have to worry about the engineers coming up with a new plan where we've got to do more work."

It's not unusual, then, to have shop workers, office workers, and even managers avoid the risk of losing their group membership. We recall the case of a middle manager who was unmarried, had no close family ties, and was thoroughly devoted to his job. In fact, he averaged sixty to seventy hours a week in the office. Higher executives marveled at this manager's interest, dedication, and eagerness, but his fellow middle managers had little to do with him because of his disregard for the group's standards.

Communications

Commonly called the grapevine, informal communications play an important role in any organization. Much informal communication is different from the grapevine, however, and is directly responsible for getting things done. Workers may seek out their informal leader for advice or their most skilled member for help on a problem, but these contacts are not shown on the formal organization chart.

Informal communications vary in their nature and volume, depending on how the formal communication system of the chain of command operates. If the formal organization is not well informed about important matters, the members seem to lean more heavily on the informal organization for information. The informal organization's communication system is most active, then, when formal channels do not provide information about matters that directly affect organization members.

In a plant that had a history of layoffs at certain times of year, the grapevine promptly went to work when the plant manager announced that some older equipment was to be replaced. The plant began to buzz with stories about how the new equipment would replace certain employees, and these informal communications not only seriously hampered workers' efficiency and morale but caused several to quit and take jobs with another firm. It was some time before top management recognized what had happened and promptly put an end to the rumor by formally announcing that no employees would lose their jobs.

We frequently have informal communications about pay raises, layoffs, promotions, transfers, and factors most critical to our need satisfaction—these are the most highly active grapevine matters. However, this does not mean that the informal communication systems are alive only when the formal system is not; they are always alive, and frequently support or discredit communications carried through formal channels. For example, the formal oganization channels may carefully explain that new machinery in the above example will bring lower job costs and safer working conditions and that no worker will be laid off because of the new equipment. But the informal organization can carry information that directly discredits formal communications. The grapevine may carry information that workers displaced by the new equipment will be given dirty, routinized, lower status jobs, or that they will be kept for awhile, then released. Thus, the informal communication system may add to, take from, or reinforce formal communications.

One study found that staff personnel tended to be more in the know regarding informal communications than were line management personnel.[4] This seems logical, because many staff positions require movement and interactions with personnel in departments other than their own. It was also found that some individuals were more frequently involved in informal communications and served as a liaison in relaying information from group to group. This service definitely enhances the status of these liaison people as well as providing informal group members information about matters that interest or affect them.

A manager must definitely be aware of the part that the grapevine plays in organizations. The less he informs his subordinates about matters they consider important, the more he is inviting the informal communication system to generate, correctly or incorrectly, information about these matters.

WORKING WITH THE INFORMAL ORGANIZATION

A manager must respect informal organization or be willing to pay a price. He must recognize it, and most important, he must understand it. Management cannot create informal organization nor can it abolish it (though many managers would love to do so), but it can influence it by recognizing group leaders or by, for example, determining who will work with whom and where.

But however hard a supervisor may try to work with his informal group, poor working conditions, low pay, and an untrustworthy top management can create circumstances where a lower level supervisor has little chance of using the informal group to help him accomplish his department's objectives. Restricted output, informal group resistance, and other such behavior may not be aimed at the immediate supervisor but at top management. For example, a sales supervisor may find that his salaried salesmen respect a group standard of an average number of calls to be made during the week. The salesmen may distrust top sales management and feel that the number of calls required might be drastically increased if they were to show evidence of really putting out for their own supervisor.

Thus, we frequently find the individual supervisor caught in the middle of two conflicting interests (Figure 15). To carry out formal organization demands will only alienate his subordinates and run counter to their wishes. To pacify the informal organization may not allow him to accomplish the formal objectives of the organization. Frequently, the acceptable action is a compromise. But the individual supervisor can definitely be handicapped in his relations with his informal group when top management is perceived to be untrustworthy and unfair.

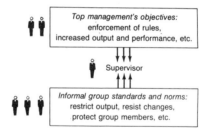

Figure 15.   The individual supervisor caught in conflicting interests.

Working with the Informal Leader

Being able to identify the informal leader (or leaders) in his group and work with him can be extremely helpful to a manager. Usually an informal group leader can be identified because he acts as a spokesman for his group, influences their opinions at meetings, or in other ways causes the group to look up to him.

When an informal leader can be identified (it is sometimes difficult), it is often fruitful for the manager to seek out his ideas about the group's thinking. For example, here is how one manager approached the informal leader of his work group about an antici- pated change in work procedure: "Bill, I'd like to get your views on what the men will think of the possibility of a new reporting system in writing up their sales calls. The boss asked my opinion, and I told him I'd let him know. I realize that we have a lot of paper work now, but this new system seems badly needed in helping us get an idea of how we can best concentrate our sales effort. What are your feelings on this thing, and what do you think the other men feel about it?" An advantage of this approach is that it is easier to work with one man than with an entire group. If the informal leader can be won over, or can make a positive contribu- tion to a plan in some way, a strong step will be taken toward his group's acceptance of it.

Not all informal leaders are necessarily so eager to work with management. One may be recognized as an informal leader by his group primarily because of his ability to outwit and resist management. To be asked to work closely with management, and to do so, would certainly jeopardize his position of leadership with his group. There is usually some explanation as to why the work group identifies and accepts such an informal leader in the first place. For example, the supervisor could make unfair demands, discipline poorly, and treat workers harshly. Or perhaps top management itself is distrusted. When these problems are remedied, the informal leader and the work group will begin to accept management's goals and work in harmony.

Selecting Work Groups

Many work situations require close cooperation among work mem- bers. A supervisor's choices in making task assignments can affect the group's overall performance. In one study of seventy-four car- penters and bricklayers on a large construction project, each worker was asked to pick the person he would like to work with most. Pairs of workers were selected on this basis, and then groups of four workers were selected in the same way. During the eleven- month period after the teams were organized, the overall result was happier, with more satisfied workers and a saving of 5 percent in total production costs.[5]

Thus, a supervisor should consider the informal forces that

exist among individuals in his department. We have seen cases where isolated workers—who for one reason or another were not accepted into the informal group—were assigned work stations close to each other, and this frequently encouraged companionship and the formation of a subgroup of their own, whereas previously they were looked upon as and felt like "isolates."

One thing we can say with certainty—informal organization and informal groups are bound to exist. And the manager who accepts this fact can then turn his attention toward learning to harness its energy. This has been well stated by authors Strauss and Sayles as follows:

> The freedom of any given set of supervisors and subordinates to develop a cooperative relationship may be limited by economic considerations, top management policy, general union-management relations, and other environmental factors. Still the attitude of the work group toward the supervisor is to a large extent a function of his attitude toward the group. If the supervisor tries to meet the expectations of his subordinates, they will be more likely to work with him.
>
> In a way, the effective supervisor acts like an informal leader. He behaves in the way his subordinates think a good leader should. He respects the group standards of conduct and value. He consults with his subordinates before taking action and encourages them to make their own decisions. In handling group problems, he either meets with the group as a whole or channels his activity through the group's informal structure (of leadership or status). He tries to build the group into a smooth, cohesive work team. . . . These techniques cannot guarantee willing group acceptance of management's objectives, but they do make it more likely.[6]

SUMMARY

The informal organization, while not shown in formal organization charts, nevertheless has many characteristics of formal organizations. Its characteristics are leadership, status, standards and norms, discipline, and communication. Informal organizations arise from man's desire to feel "included" as part of a group. The informal organization's goals do not always run counter to the objectives of the formal organization. Management must make a conscious effort to work with the informal organization, for the informal organization is a fact of organizational life.

QUESTIONS

1. List some of the organizations you belong to—either formal groups such as a fraternity or official campus organizations or less formal groups such as your classmates in a course which you are taking. Are the informal leaders identifiable? How do they display leadership?

2. A manager reading this chapter remarks, "This informal organization stuff is a bunch of bunk. Sure, people get together and talk about things over coffee break or lunch, or even on the job. But there's only one group in this company that determines our goals, objectives, and standards, and that's top management. This informal organization is strictly overrated by the human relations people, if you ask me." Discuss.

3. When a vacancy occurs in a supervisory position, some companies make a practice of promoting the informal work leader to fill the vacancy. What are the disadvantages and advantages of this approach?

4. Why do companies have formal organization charts when the "informal organization" describes "the way things really get done in an organization"?

5. Recalling the characteristics of informal organizations such as status, communications, standards and norms, and discipline, think back to jobs have held or presently hold in formal organizations. How were some of these characteristics of informal organization displayed?

6. Is it possible for the informal and formal organization of a particular goal seeking group to be identical?

NOTES

1. See F. J. Roethlisberger and William Dickson, *Management and the Worker: An Account of a Research Program Conducted by the Western Electric Company, Hawthorne Works, Chicago* (Cambridge, Mass.: Harvard University Press, 1939, 1967). Copyright 1939, 1967 by the President and Fellows of Harvard College.
2. *Ibid.*, p. 525.
3. *Ibid.*, p. 383.
4. Keith Davis, "Management Communication and the Grapevine," *Harvard Business Review*, September-October, 1953, pp. 43–49.
5. R. H. Van Zelst, "Sociometrically Selected Work Teams Increase Production," *Personnel Psychology*, Autumn 1952, pp., 175–85.
6. George Strauss and Leonard Sayles, *Personnel: The Human Problems of Management*, 3rd ed. (Englewood Cliffs, N. J.: Prentice-Hall, 1972), p. 183.

7

Management Communication: A Difficult Task

If we had to select one skill that contributes to a manager's effectiveness, it would be his understanding of communication with others. In a typical manager's work day, he makes assignments, provides information, corrects subordinates' errors, discusses problems with staff departments, reports accomplishments to his superiors, attends meetings, listens to and counsels subordinates—the list could go on and on. It is not unusual, then, that studies show that the typical manager spends from 60 to 80 percent of his time in communication. Because of the importance of communication and the span of activities it covers, we will give two chapters to it, this one on the problems and barriers to communication, the next one on what a manager can do to use communication more effectively.

Communication is like the blood that keeps the body of the organization functioning. What, for example, unifies, binds, and directs the efforts of over 800,000 General Motors employees in working toward goals and objectives? Obviously, a very complex system of coordination and communication holds this organization giant together.

As Figure 16 shows, a tremendous volume of communication constantly flows from top management down to lower organizational levels: policy announcements, decisions, procedures, authority delegations, and general information. Flowing upward is information on sales volume, production reports, problem areas, new developments, and grievances. Flowing *laterally* and *diagonally* within the organization is a different kind of information: reports between departments needing to coordinate efforts such as credit reports furnished to salesmen; communications between various production departments such as fabricating, assembly, and packing; sales orders for production departments; problem-solving conferences of managers from various levels and departments; and advice and information flowing between line and staff departments. Figure 16, then, shows why communication is so important to an organization's overall effectiveness, as well as to the individual manager who uses communication so heavily in his work day.

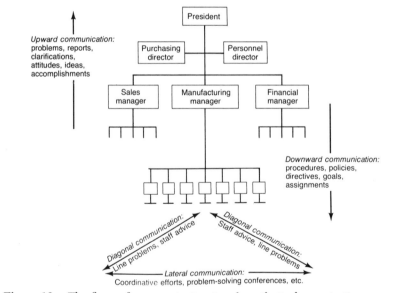

Figure 16.   The flows of communication in a hypothetical organization.

FOUR PIONEERS IN MANAGEMENT COMMUNICATION: FAYOL, FOLLETT, CARNEGIE, BARNARD

Despite the generally acknowledged importance of communication today, its role was not always so fully respected. In fact, the term "communication" was hardly ever used in organizations prior to the 1950s. Let us now take a look at four people who helped us recognize its importance: *Henri Fayol*, considered by many to be the outstanding single contributor to the management field; psychologist *Mary Parker Follett*, credited with gradually bringing the "human relations" approach to management; *Dale Carnegie*, best known of the four, who approached communication from the applied viewpoint of the typical businessman; and *Chester Barnard*, a giant in management and organization theory.

Henri Fayol: The Bridge of Horizontal Communication

The first significant reference to communication in organizations is found in the work of Frenchman Henri Fayol, who along with an American, Frederick Taylor, is generally credited with making the greatest contribution to the development of a "science" of management. In 1916 Fayol recognized the problem of sending a communication through every link in the managerial chain of command: "This path is dictated both by the need for some transmission and by the principle of unity of command, but it is not always the swiftest. It is even at times disastrously lengthy in large concerns, notably in governmental ones. Now, there are many activities whose success turns on speedy execution, hence respect for the line of authority must be reconciled with the need for swift action. . . . It is an error to depart needlessly from the line of authority, but it is an even greater one to keep to it when detrimental to the business concern."[1]

Fayol thus proposed a precept of *horizontal communication*. This idea recognized that it was often best to have direct *lateral* communication between members of separate organization levels rather than to stick strictly with the chain of command. As Figure 17 shows, a plant manager might have two subordinates—a production manager and a quality-control manager. Each in turn has three subordinates of his own: the production manager has three foremen and the quality-control manager has three inspectors. Suppose an inspector must communicate a message to one of the foremen regarding some faulty work that did not pass inspection standards. Strict compliance with the chain of command dictates that he would relay his message to his own superior, the quality-control manager, who would relay it up to the plant manager, who would relay it down to the production manager, who would relay it to the foreman. Thus, the message would have to pass through three persons.

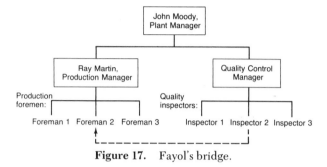

Figure 17. Fayol's bridge.

Fayol contended that, in such a case, strict compliance with the chain of command was too slow, that the inspector should *bridge* the communication—communicate directly with the foreman—since it would be not only quicker but more accurate. However, the basic rule to be followed is that the inspector and foreman should keep their superiors informed, and even get permission first to handle routine problems directly.

Many of Fayol's other principles and concepts have remained as the foundation for management theory today, and "Fayol's Bridge" is also popularly known by students of management.

Mary Parker Follett: The Giving of Orders

In 1925, psychologist Mary Parker Follett presented a paper entitled "The Giving of Orders," an activity that in those days managers did by instinct rather than as a result of careful thought. Miss Follett noted that many managers gave orders poorly and that this had a negative effect upon employees: "To some men," she wrote, "the matter of giving orders seems a very simple affair; they expect to issue their orders and have them obeyed without question. Yet on the other hand, the shrewd common sense of many a business executive has shown him that the giving of orders is surrounded by many difficulties; that to demand an unquestioning obedience to orders not approved, not perhaps even understood, is bad business policy. Moreover, psychology, as well as our own observation, shows us only that you cannot get people to do things most satisfactorily by ordering them or exhorting them."[2]

When an order is given in a manner disagreeable to the subordinate, she argued, he feels his self-respect attacked and becomes defensive. Thus, he is hardly in a frame of mind to carry out his work well. Actually, there should be no reason for a superior to play the role of a dictator in giving orders to his workers. Miss Follett felt that, ideally, a worker will accept and carry out his superior's orders and assignments as long as they are felt by the worker to be fair. A manager's orders, if fair, are accepted by his subordinates as simply a normal part of the situation that brings a boss and his subordinate together. Obviously, Miss Follett's views of the giving of orders are appropriate even today.

Dale Carnegie: Communication Training for Managers

Dale Carnegie courses today are among the widest known of all professional improvement programs. The course is offered in almost every large city of the United States, and many organizations gladly pay the tuition fees for their employees to enroll. Back in the 1920s when Carnegie's writings and courses were first becoming popular, he argued that there was a direct link between a manager's communication skills and his success.

Emphasizing such skills as speaking, listening, and good human relations through communication, Carnegie's courses created the first large-scale awareness that a business and its managers must be effective communicators to be successful. "How to win friends and influence people," the basic premise that Carnegie's course holds out, has attracted people from all walks of life, including salesmen, public-relations personnel, clergymen, as well as managers and executives.

Chester Barnard: The First Executive Function

A fourth pioneer in management communication was Chester Barnard, who wrote in his 1938 management classic, *The Functions of the Executive*, that "the first executive function is to develop and maintain a system of communication."³ One of Barnard's main contributions is his theory of authority in organizations. He looked on a system of authority as essentially a communication process. You can see this clearly in some of his rules for a good system of authority:

1. Channels of communication should be definitely known. Clearly established lines of authority should be developed

through practice and habit, by making official appoint-
ments well known and by using organization charts.

2. Formal channels of communication should exist for everyone in the organization. Every employee must report to
someone and therefore be subordinate to someone.

3. The competence of the persons serving as communication
centers (officers, supervisory heads, and managers) must
be adequate.

4. Every communication must be authenticated; that is, the
person communicating must be known to occupy the
position of ability concerned.

5. The greater the number of levels of authority in an organization, the slower and less accurate is communication that
flows from the top of the organization downward through
each level.[4]

WHAT COMMUNICATION IS: A FIVE-STAGE MODEL

Now that we have mentioned some of the highlights that helped
make communication a more popular concern of managers, let us
turn to the subject ourselves. How is communication defined?
What are some major barriers to it? How do organizations compli-
cate a manager's effectiveness in communicating? Why is it more
difficult to communicate with subordinates than with, say, the
average person on the street?

Many managers do not understand what is meant by the term
communication. They think it covers only what a manager says or
writes, or that which is intentional on his part, when in fact it can
include broader things such as what he does, his dress, and his
behavior.

Consider the example of George, office manager in a large
company, who was perplexed as to how he might get through to
Mary, a new eighteen-year-old employee who was not responding
to her training as he had hoped. The girl seemed to have excellent
credentials, but it was her first full-time job and she repeated many
of the same mistakes, even though each day George would go over
her previous day's work with her. What upset George most was
the girl's extreme nervousness in his presence. Early one day as
Mary entered George's office, the door slammed loudly behind
her. She hurriedly began to apologize. However, George ex-

plained that the door always slammed because of a draft in the office, especially in the morning because he usually forgot to fasten it open.

That afternoon, a clerk who had worked in the office for several years came up to George. "George," he said, "Mary just had us in stitches over in the coffee lounge. She told us about how the door slammed on her this morning. Do you know that door had really given her a complex? She said every morning would start off with you coming into your office, slamming the door, and shortly afterwards asking her to come into your office to go over her previous day's work. She was scared to death of you every morning!"

Is it communication when George unknowingly slams the door and creates Mary's tenseness? Actually, it can be called such. A manager must be concerned that subordinates or other members of the organization *respond properly* to his leadership, instructions, or persuasion *in the way he intends.* Thus, he must also be conscious of those things he does unintentionally which may conflict with his intentional behavior. The unconscious, unintended door slamming overshadowed the effect of George's intended communication to Mary.

Communication, then, is the process by which people exchange facts, ideas, opinions, emotions, or feelings. When a person receives an impression from something you have said or done, you have communicated to him, whether you are aware of it or not. To appreciate how complex communication is, let us examine Figure 18 on the next page. There are five stages.

Stage 1—An Event Occurs. Here all of the stimuli associated with the happening of a given event occur. These stimuli consist generally of factors capable of causing a response or making an impact on someone. For example, When a manager gives a subordinate instructions the basic stimuli consist of the sounds of the manager's words, his facial expressions, movements, and dress.

Stage 2—Senses Receive. This stage shows that the first person's senses (Mr. A's) have picked up some of the stimuli that occurred with the event in stage 1; his senses of sight, hearing, touch, taste, and smell have come into play. His senses are bombarded by stimuli. Because of man's sensory limitations, however, he cannot possibly pick up all of the stimuli associated with a given event. For example, when you look at a picture of, say, a street

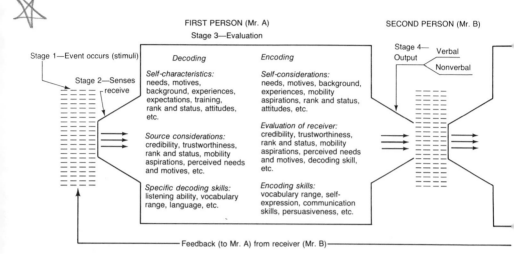

Figure 18. The process of communication. (Adapted from W. Johnson, "The Fateful Process of Mr. A Talking to Mr. B," *Harvard Business Review*, January-February, 1953, p. 50.)

scene, many fine details will escape you—the number of cars or exactly what each object or person looks like. Similarly, when a subordinate receives instructions from his boss, he may not pick up certain facial expressions, variations in quality and tone of voice, details of what the boss was wearing, gestures used, and so on. He will probably concentrate primarily on the words the boss uses, since the subordinate will consider them most important.

Stage 3—Evaluation. The stimuli received by the senses are carried quickly to the brain, where they are first given meaning— that is, *decoded*. How we decode depends upon three factors. First are *self-characteristics*—our needs, motives, education, culture, attitudes, and so on. Second are *source considerations*—whether we think the source of the message is believable, trustworthy, has authority, and so on. Third are *skill factors*—our listening ability, vocabulary range, and level of language comprehension. After decoding, we evaluate what our response to the stimuli will be and the thoughts received are converted into a response—that is, *encoded*. How we encode also depends on three factors. First are the same *self-characteristics* (our needs, motives, and so on) we used in decoding. Second are *receiver characteristics*—whether we think the receiver of our message is to be trusted, what we think his level of understanding is, how much authority he has, whether he appears to be motivated by ego, security, or challenge. Third are *skill factors*—our flexibility with vocabulary, ability to express ideas, and knowledge and skill in persuasion techniques. For example, when a subordinate receives instructions from a manager, he decodes them in terms of his past work experience, knowledge of the job, and so on. If he does not understand the instructions, however, evaluation of his intended receiver is critically important. If his boss appears to be an open and receptive person, the subordinate may prepare a message such as, "Will you go over it one more time?" or, "What exactly do I do with that order again?" But if the subordinate knows that his boss tends to become irritated by questions, he may say "I follow you all the way, sir," when in fact he may not. Thus, the receiver's evaluation of the sender of the message and the sender's evaluation of who his receiver is are critical determinants of interpersonal communication.

Stage 4—Output. This stage consists of the actual verbal and nonverbal responses we make to the stimuli that we initially received and evaluated. Output, which may be either intentional or unintentional, consists of words, movements, gestures, facial expressions, and any other type of response that we make.

Stage 5—New Event Occurs. This stage consists of the stimuli associated with sounds, movements, and expressions of Stage 4. As shown in the model, then, the cycle of communication begins again. Person B will pick up the stimuli sent by Mr. A, decode it, then encode his response to Mr. A. The new stimuli will take the form of feedback to Mr. A, and is shown by the line at the bottom of the model.

ORGANIZATIONAL AND INTERPERSONAL BARRIERS TO MANAGEMENT COMMUNICATION

With the above understanding of the communication process, let us explore some typical communication barriers that confront the manager in his interactions with others.

Organizations have three factors in common which tend to create problems in communication among their members: (1) levels of hierarchy, (2) managerial authority, and (3) specialization.

Levels of Hierarchy

As organizations grow, their structure expands to accommodate the burden of directing additional or broadened activities of their members, as happened with John Moody's boat-trailer company in Chapter 2. Although such growth is necessary for many organizations, it still leads to more communication problems. If a message must pass through increased levels, two things will happen: it will take longer for the message to reach its destination and the message will tend to become less accurate.

As a message goes up or down levels of hierarchy, it passes through a number of "substations," each with its unique perceptions, motives, needs, and relationships with the nature of the message. Each level in the communication chain can add to, take from, qualify, or change completely the intent of a given message (see Figure 19). One study of 100 companies found a drop-off in

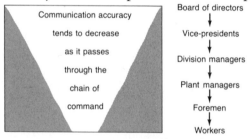

Figure 19.   Loss of information in the chain of command.

communication accuracy as a message went from top to bottom: the vice-presidential level understood 67 percent of what it heard from the board of directors; at the division manager level, 56 percent of the same information survived; at the plant manager level, 40 percent survived; at the foreman level, 30 percent and at the operating level, only 20 percent.[5]

One major explanation for the cause of such a loss of information in organizations is that at higher levels of management, messages are usually broader and more general. However, at lower levels these same messages must be implemented and put into specific use. As Barnard notes, communications are likely to be expressed in more general terms the more general and higher the position. "It follows," he adds, "that something may be lost or added by transmission at each stage of the process, especially when communication is oral, or when at each stage there is a combination of several communications. Moreover, when communications go from high positions down they often must be made more specific as they proceed."[6]

Thus, at any level in the hierarchy, a given communication may be understood fully, partially, or not at all. Each level has as communication barriers: (1) its own limiting knowledge about the subject or message content; (2) its own frame of reference from which it interprets the message; (3) previous inaccuracies that might have been passed down the chain of command and that accompany the message itself; and (4) inaccuracies that are carried through the grapevine.

Managerial Authority

Authority is a necessary feature of an organization, and it would be impossible to accomplish much without certain persons having the right to make decisions. Yet, the very fact that one person is a boss figure over others creates a barrier to free and open communications. No doubt you have heard subordinates complain about a boss somewhat as follows: "You know, this idea of his is just plain crazy. The thing won't work now, and even if we work on it all year it'll still never develop. But when he says do it, we have to do it. I remember what happened when Adamson told him the truth about one of his bright new ideas. You have to go along with things that come down from the top, and by God, when the old man asks for an opinion, you'd better tell him what he wants to hear." Thus, subordinates tend to communicate to their superior the kind of information he is most apt to welcome. Job problems, frustrations, below-standard work, disagreements with the superior's policies, and other unfavorable information tends to be withheld from him or changed to look more favorable.

One study of a department run by an autocratic superintendent found that his middle-management supervisors spent a lot of time complaining among themselves, but in his presence they tended to pretend that they were all one happy, hard-working team and that everything was going fine. They also kept to a minimum any communication with the boss that he might take as pressure and tended to communicate information that might be detrimental to others and favorable to themselves, thereby furthering their competitive cause for the boss's good graces.[7]

A superior's authority and status over his subordinates even affects *his* communications with his own subordinates. Many superiors feel that they cannot fully admit those problems, conditions, or results that may make them look weak. As a result there is a lack of "leveling" between boss and subordinates.

Specialization

Specialization, or division of labor, is a fundamental part of organizations. This principle holds that greater worker efficiency results when a person does only one or certain aspects of the task—accountants doing accounting, salesmen doing selling, engineers doing efficiency studies, and so on. But specialization also creates problems. As one observer puts it, specialization "tends to separate people even when they work side by side. Differences in function, special interest, and job jargon can make people feel that they live in different worlds. The result . . . drowns out community of feeling and makes understanding very difficult."[8]

Obviously, one common problem created by specialization is the "jargon" or technical words of the trade that are used by various specialists. We have seen much resistance to data-processing departments because of the technical language that data-processing specialists use. But even deeper than the problem of language are the differing perceptions and conflicting frames of reference involved where sales, credit, production, quality control, finance, and research departments interact regarding company policies. These departments have their own subgroup loyalties, interests, attitudes, and ways of looking at things which frequently create strains between individuals and departments.

Even if organizational communication barriers did not exist, would a manager still be able to communicate without any worries about his message going awry? Unfortunately, many daily miscommunications are caused not by organizational factors, but by problems of language or of human imperfections. A manager must also be aware of these interpersonal barriers.

Differing Perceptions Between Sender and Receiver

Perception is a complicated process by which we select, organize, and give meaning to the world around us. It is like the decoding stage of the communication model that we discussed earlier.

Since humans are organizing animals, as soon as we perceive something, we organize it into some type of meaningful whole. We learn to hear a train whistle, and we expect to see a train; to be dealt a black ace of hearts, but still "see" it as red; to be called into the boss's office, and to automatically become defensive. In other words, our expectations force into certain categories the events, people, objects, and situations we daily encounter. That our expectations influence what we see and hear was shown in one study in which, by subtle devices, some members of an audience were given the suggestion that the guest speaker was a warm and friendly person and others received the suggestion that he was cold and distant. Later, when the audience rated the speaker's talk, it is found that most members—who heard the identical speech—"heard" the speech in such a way as to agree with their initial expectations.[9]

This tendency to structure our world into such a pattern creates *stereotyping*. Blacks, union leaders, and staff experts, for instance, may be categorized because of one or several apparent similarities, and individual differences may be completely unnoticed. One manager may label all blacks as lazy, all union leaders agitators, and all staff people "a bunch of meddlers." As one writer puts it, "If a union representative comes to deal with a personnel manager on a grievance, he brings an expectancy based on certain past experiences with personnel managers. He assumes that certain kinds of behavior and certain attitudes will be manifest in the situation. Because a new man has the role of personnel manager, the representative tends to assimilate this new experience into the preexisting pattern and to act as if this executive was like all others. He finds it difficult to deal with the new personnel manager as an individual, a new and fundamentally different person."[10]

One limiting factor in our perception is that we cannot grasp the whole of a stimulus at a given instant of time. Some parts of an event receive greater attention than do others, some receive none at all. Those we do focus on usually serve some immediate purpose. Our needs, moods, cultural and social influences, and attitudes all interact to determine which stimuli are important and to determine the role we assign to them. In a factory accident, for example, all those involved will "see" the accident differently: the foreman (who has just lost a valuable worker), the safety engineer (whose safety record has been blemished), the fellow worker (who is best friends with the injured worker), the company physician (who attends the injured worker), and the personnel manager (who is concerned with workmen's compensation and finding a replacement for the injured worker). If each person were to communicate about the accident, the different versions would be colored by those stimuli selected.

A second limiting factor is that when we perceive an object or person, our evaluation is frequently colored by the larger properties of which that object or person is a part. The way a subordinate "looks at" his boss and his boss's messages is not influenced just by his relationship with his boss. The overall attitude of the subordinate toward management in general (of which his boss is part) also plays a significant part. Much depends upon the subordinate's seeing his boss as a submember of a larger structure bearing the label "management."

Thus, a communicator should allow for three distinct aspects of perception: (1) the person who is the receiver will interpret the message in terms of *his* own experience and the ways he has learned to respond to it; (2) the receiver will interpret the message in such a way as to resist any change in strong personality structures; and (3) the receiver will tend to group characteristics of his experience so as to make whole patterns. Thus, as Wilbur Schramm, a great student of mass communication, points out: "The moral for the manager trying to get his message across is . . . that one must know as much as possible about the frames of reference, needs, goals, languages, and stereotypes of his receiver, if he hopes to get his meaning across."[11]

Receiver's Evaluation of Communicator

A major communication barrier lies in the tendency of a communication receiver to size up, evaluate, and weigh a message in terms of the characteristics of the person who sends it. We will focus here on two characteristics of the communicator—his credibility and his trustworthiness.

Research has shown that we are more likely to accept a given message when we have a favorable attitude toward the sender. When a manager is seen as having a high credibility rating, his subordinates are more likely to accept his communications, other things being equal. The late Yale professor Carl Hovland found that, in general, whether we accept a persuasive message or not is conditioned by the way we size up the communicator.[12] A communicator's credibility is based, first on his "expertness" in the subject area being communicated and, second, on our degree of confidence or trust that he will communicate the truth.

There are three possible reasons why we do not tend to accept messages from less credible communicators. First, we tend not to expose ourselves to communication from sources toward whom we have negative attitudes. Second, because of unfavorable attitudes, we do not pay close attention to the content and/or do not attempt to understand what is being said. Third, because of our unfavorable attitudes toward a speaker, we are not motivated to accept or believe what he says. It follows, then, that a manager must be viewed as credible and trustworthy by his subordinates. Otherwise, his communication attempts to motivate, persuade, and direct the work efforts of his subordinates are greatly handicapped.

Defensiveness

A feeling of defensiveness on the part of a message sender, receiver, or both creates a severe communication barrier. Defensiveness by one person causes certain facial expressions, bodily movements, and speech which in turn increases the defense level of the other party. Thus, a defensive chain reaction begins. This defensive listening causes each of us to concentrate more on what we will say than on what we hear. When we feel defensive, we also distort what we do receive; we are not as likely to accurately perceive the motives, values, and emotions of our receiver.

There are six situations that are likely to arouse defensiveness, according to one scholar, and therefore present greater built-in communication barriers to managers.

1. *Evaluation* includes passing judgment on another, blaming, praising—for example, when a manager corrects his subordinate's errors or calls them to his attention, or the more formal performance appraisal or merit rating of past performance.
2. *Control* includes attempts to change attitudes or behavior.

Many performance appraisals also fall into this category, as would disciplinary interviews, attempts to change attitudes toward the job, the department, or the organization, and efforts to get subordinates to accept forthcoming changes.

3. *Strategy* includes attempts to use tricks to involve others, to make them feel more important. When subordinates see through a manager's use of democratic leadership as a gimmick or strategy to make them feel more involved, defensive behavior results.

4. *Neutrality* includes a superior's obvious lack of concern for his subordinates' welfare. This would include statements or actions on the manager's part which indicate a detached, uninvolved disregard for subordinates.

5. *Superiority* includes situations where the superior is perceived by others as behaving in a pompous or "better than thou" manner, displaying status, power, ability, or intellect in a way that obviously calls attention to feelings of inadequacy in subordinates.

6. *Certainty* includes situations where superiors seem to know all the answers, cannot tolerate disagreement from subordinates, and feel it unnecessary to gather additional facts or information in drawing conclusions and making decisions.[13]

Because a manager has authority and status over his subordinates, he must be especially aware of those situations most likely to make them feel defensive.

Poor Listening Habits

Research seems to show that we listen at about 50 percent efficiency in terms of immediate recall and only about 25 percent at the end of two months. Among poor listening habits are (1) listening only on the surface, with little attempt to seriously consider what the other person says; (2) through either speech or manner appearing anxious to end the conversation (glancing at watch, staring into space, fidgeting); (3) showing signs of annoyance or distress over the subject matter being discussed; and (4) inactive listening, failing to understand the frame of reference of the person speaking.

But more basic than acquiring good listening habits is a manager's attitude toward listening. Is he willing to spend the time? Does he make himself available? His attitude toward listening plays the most important role in determining whether a system of upward communication exists.

Because we all naturally defend our actions, superiors as well as subordinates resent unfavorable communication. Also, many superiors are reluctant to listen in order to avoid becoming involved in a subordinate's personal problems. However, not listening in one case may affect subordinates' willingness to communicate job-related problems at a future date. Finally, since listening consumes time, a manager's having too large a span of control subsequently limits his listening opportunities.

Impreciseness of Language

One of the biggest mistakes we make in communicating is to assume that meaning lies with the "words" we use. For example, a supervisor who tells his subordinate to "clean up around here," and means only a five-minute clean-up of scraps near the worker's drill press, will be quite distressed to return an hour later to find the worker still "cleaning up" the entire department area at the expense of a backlog of production work. To blame the worker for the communication breakdown may protect the supervisor's ego, but it represents a poor approach toward a manager's communication responsibilities. Unless the manager recognizes that the meaning of the words he uses is really dependent upon *his* *receiver* (and not his own words), he will most likely see all communication breakdowns as "the other guy's fault."

Earlier in the chapter we mentioned that each person has a separate set of experiences, training, background, and so on, which causes highly individual interpretations of what he sees and hears. Words also can arouse feelings, emotions, and attitudes within people. This is what we refer to as the *connotative* meaning of a word, as compared to its dictionary definition. Thus, the foreman who says "Well, boys, let's get on with this job" may be unaware that the term "boys" is strongly offensive to black workers, though it carries no such connotation to white workers. And the dictionary definition of "boy" seems harmless enough. Yet to black workers, the term frequently connotes servanthood or calls attention to lower status. We have known of many cases where managers have used this term unwittingly and have been "tuned out" by many of their black workers.

A study by the Opinion Research Corporation of Princeton, New Jersey, investigated the impact of sixty-one commonly used terms by management upon 488 industrial hourly paid employees. The word *capitalism* as harmlessly used by management connoted to these workers such feelings as "the wealthiest people take over," "big business has so much money they freeze out the little fellow," or "a dictatorship by the rich." The word *corporation* aroused a strong image of money, power, and selfishness; *company* was much more favorably accepted. The term *work stoppage* was identified as an unfairness; however, *strike* was accepted as a practical, fair means to an end.[14]

Another study found that terms such as *closed shop, grievance, seniority,* and *labor movement* have different connotations for members of labor and management and create a severe communications barrier between the two groups.[15] Even at various levels of management, words such as *quota, budget,* and *performance appraisal* may have different meanings at each level. Whereas a superior may speak of performance appraisal as a means of providing development, improvement, and growth for his subordinate, the subordinate may resent the term as an unnecessary process designed only to satisfy his boss's power and status needs. Thus, when the two parties refer to the term, each is on a separate wavelength.

The fact that meaning lies within the users of words, rather than the words themselves places a tremendous burden upon each manager to anticipate the connotative meanings that his subordinates give to words. Like all humans, the manager is also victimized by the impreciseness of language.

Nonverbal Barriers

The incident we showed earlier of the impact George's unintentional door slamming had on his subordinate's behavior is an example of how communication is not confined to just words.

A manager must also be aware of the impact of three types of non-verbal behavior which might also be communication barrier—sign language, action language, and object language. *Sign language* takes the form of gestures of motions, such as the pointed hand, and actually replaces words. *Action language* includes all bodily movements or expressions that communicate but that are not primarily intended for communicative purposes—for example, facial expression, posture, or George's door slamming. *Object language* includes the display of material things, such as thick carpet, large desk, or formal reception room.[16]

The importance of nonverbal factors becomes obvious when we realize that they frequently contradict what we say. Since much nonverbal communication is unintentional, it poses an especially difficult problem. Within the superior-subordinate setting, nonverbal communication barriers may be shown in lack of interest, poor eye contact, and disturbing physical mannerisms. Or they may take a more subtle form of object language and be essentially status related; for example, a superior may sit with his back to the light, continue to write when a subordinate enters the room, use a chair just a little higher than that of his visitor, make others feel insecure by use of formal office surroundings such as thick carpets, large desk, or fancy wallpaper.

SUMMARY

This chapter pointed out that communication is a relatively new term in management. Four early management pioneers, however, recognized its importance to management a number of years ago. Henri Fayol saw the merits of horizontal communication with his "bridge" in 1916. Mary Parker Follett in the 1920s publicized the importance of communication in superior-subordinate relations, especially in the superior's giving of orders. Dale Carnegie in the 1920s emphasized the importance of communication through his popular training courses, promising managers personal effectiveness through better communication skills. Chester Barnard in 1938 saw the entire organizational system as a communication chain.

A number of possibilities for communication arise in organizations, complicating the manager's communication task. These are organizational barriers, such as levels of hierarchy, authority, and specialization, and interpersonal barriers, such as differing perceptions, defensiveness, poor listening habits, imprecise language, and nonverbal factors.

A five-stage communication model was presented which showed how complex the communication process really is when Person A passes information to Person B. Stage 1 represents the stimuli associated with an event. In Stage 2, Mr. A's senses receive the stimuli; in Stage 3, the stimuli are evaluated. Stage 4 consists of the response to stimuli, and Stage 5 becomes new stimuli to Person B. The stages are repeated within Person B, and his response becomes feedback to Person A.

QUESTIONS

1. "Communication may be defined as the process by which a message sender converts his thoughts into words and symbols, forwards them to his receiver, where a satisfactory interpretation is made." How does this definition of communication differ from that made in the chapter?

2. A management expert talking with a group of top executives states "The mere fact that organization exists means an automatic *tendency* for it to have certain communication problems. You show me any organization chart and I'll show you some automatic communication problems that exist to some extent or another." What are these communication problems he is referring to?

3. What is the difference between connotative and dictionary meaning? Give some examples of words that may have different connotations for you and some of your classmates or fellow workers.

4. Some managers are firm believers of "putting it in writing." Others favor oral, face-to-face communication. What are the relative strengths and weaknesses of the two types of communication?

5. Chapter 3 presented Maslow's "hierarchy of needs" concept. How is interpersonal communication the means through which a worker satisfies the following needs on the job? (a) self-fulfillment needs; (b) ego or esteem needs; (c) social needs; (d) safety or security needs; (e) physiological needs.

NOTES

1. Henri Fayol, *General and Industrial Management*, translated by Constance Storrs (New York: Pittman Publishing Corp., 1949), pp. 34–36.

2. Henry C. Metcalf and L. Urwick, eds., *Dynamic Administration: The Collected Papers of Mary Parker Follett* (New York: Harper & Row, 1940), p. 51.

3. Chester Barnard, *The Functions of the Executive* (Cambridge, Mass.: Harvard University Press, 1938).

4. *Ibid.*, pp. 175–81.

5. Roderick Powers, "Measuring Effectiveness of Business Communication," *Personnel Administration*, July-August, 1963, pp. 47–52.

6. Barnard, *The Functions of the Executive*, pp. 176–77.
7. Chris Argyris, *Personality and Organization* (New York: Harper & Row, 1957), pp. 159–60.
8. Paul Pigors, *Effective Communication in Industry* (New York: National Association of Manufacturers, 1949), p. 13.
9. Harold H. Kelley, "The Warm-Cold Variable in First Impressions of Persons," *Journal of Personality*, Vol XVIII (1950), pp. 431–39.
10. Ross Stagner, *Psychology of Industrial Conflict* (New York: John Wiley & Sons, 1956), p. 35
11. Wilbur Schramm, ed., *The Process and Effects of Mass Communication* (Urbana, Ill.: University of Illinois Press, 1954), p. 114.
12. Carl I. Hovland, Irving L. Janis, and Harold H. Kelley, *Communication and Persuasion: Psychological Studies of Opinion Change* (New Haven, Conn.: Yale University Press, 1953).
13. Jack R. Gibb, "Defensive Communication," *Journal of Communication*, September, 1961, pp. 141–48.
14. Martin Wright, "Do You Need Lessons in Shop Talk?" *Personnel*, July-August, 1965, pp. 60–61.
15. Carl H. Weaver, "The Quantification of the Frame of Reference in Labor-Management Communication," *Journal of Applied Psychology*, February, 1958, pp. 1–9.
16. Jurgen Ruesch and Weldon Kees, *Nonverbal Communication: Notes on the Visual Perception of Human Relations* (Berkeley, Calif.: University of California Press, 1956), p. 64.

8

Management Communication: Six Ways to Improve It

This chapter attacks the interpersonal communication problems we discussed which take place between managers and subordinates. Typically, the kind of advice one often hears for improving communication is something like "Use simple, direct language" or "Use visual aids." However, we prefer to take a more realistic approach, using six concepts that will help a manager be more effective in communicating with subordinates. The six things that you as a manager can do are (1) establish the proper climate for communicating, (2) consider the objectives of your communication, (3) be sensitive to your subordinate's patterns of evaluation, (4) make the message identify with the subordinate's self-interest, (5) be sensitive to the language you use in the message, and (6) use feedback. We will describe each of these concepts in turn.

ESTABLISH THE PROPER CLIMATE WITH YOUR EMPLOYEES

A manager does not communicate in a vacuum; his message must be considered within the overall framework of the entire superior-subordinate and superior-group relationship. A manager and his subordinate each brings a store of experiences, expectations, and attitudes into the communication event. These mental factors strongly influence the nature of the subject communicated and the meaning each person assigns to the message forwarded and received. Thus, the outcome of any given communication between a boss and his subordinate depends on the overall setting and environment that influences the communicators, and particularly the subordinate.

What type of environment best contributes to effective communication? One writer describes the ideal climate as one where the manager has "an attitude that is people rather than production centered; an open door in both action and policy, with a clear indication that effective communication shall be practiced; and a sincere interest in listening."[1]

Earlier, we mentioned that the manager's authority and status are among the organizational factors that work against a free, accurate flow of information. We also mentioned that source credibility—how expert and trustworthy the subordinate thinks his boss is—is a main factor that determines the subordinate's acceptance of a communication from his superior. If a manager is not trusted, his subordinates likely will not communicate their real feelings about a subject. We have shown further that subordinates tend to communicate more readily to their boss information that is favorable to themselves and to withhold unfavorable information. Therefore, a favorable climate for free, accurate, honest communication must overcome these tendencies.

Create a Climate of Mutual Trust

Why does trust facilitate understanding? First, when a subordinate trusts his superior, he is more willing to communicate frankly about his job problems. Second, when he trusts his superior he is less likely to distort his superior's motives and make negative assumptions about his communications.

These problems can be related to a subordinate's desires to accomplish certain goals. As one social scientist remarks, "an individual will tend to facilitate the actions of others when he perceives that their actions will be promotive of his chances of goal attainment, and will tend to obstruct the actions of others when he perceives that their actions will be [contrary] with respect to his goal attainment."[2] A manager who represents his subordinates' interests by bargaining with higher management, disciplines fairly and consistently, and respects the abilities of his men is more likely to be viewed in a trusting manner. He is looked on as a source of help and therefore a factor in helping his subordinates to reach their goals. By working in a climate where he is not overly penalized for mistakes, a subordinate is less likely to conceal information from his boss and less likely to question the trustworthiness of his superior's motives.

Deemphasize Status Barriers

Closely related to a person's authority in organizations is his status. The deemphasis of certain status symbols also helps interpersonal communication, although we can never completely eliminate status differences in an organization nor would we want to. However, the manager must understand the effect his status has upon communication. If a manager has closer interpersonal relationships with his subordinates and more job contacts with them, accepts disagreement from them, and conducts group meetings democratically, he will be viewed as a trusting, fair leader without a necessary loss of authority and status.

A consultative or participative system of management is apt to produce a better communication climate than an autocratic system. The authoritarian system emphasizes downward communication of policies, instructions, and directives, and upward communication is likely to take the form of reports and compliance with instructions. In this environment, we feel pressure to communicate to our superior what he wants to hear, and so a lack of frankness and highly filtered upward communication are apt to prevail.

Allow Opportunities for Upward Communication

A manager can encourage upward communication from his subordinates by using a number of skills, among them practicing effective listening techniques. We have seen many managers who claim to have an "open door" policy, but it is often a meaningless gesture because subordinates do not feel the manager has a sincere interest in what they really have to say. To encourage proper upward communication, a manager must be prepared to receive unpleasant news without distress, to execute reception skills as an open and perceptive listener who emphathizes with his employees. Sociologist George Homans calls the process of listening one of the essentials of leadership:

> But it is when a follower comes to him that the leader's real work begins, and it *is* work . . . For the hardest thing in the world for a man to do is to keep his mouth shut, and that is just what the leader must do: he must listen. . . . The leader must not take a moral stand and show approval and disapproval of what is said. . . . The greatest barrier to free communication between follower and leader is the leader's authority. . . . If therefore, the leader, while he is listening to the follower, takes a moral stand or threatens to take action, he is bringing back the weight of authority, which is just what he wants to lift for the time being. . . . The encouragement of free communication on one occasion will lead to still freer communication on another.[4]

What Homans cautions against, therefore, is the leader interrupting or threatening the subordinate *before* attempting to hear entirely what the subordinate is saying.

To create a proper climate of upward communication, the superior must also be effective in communicating downwards. "The effectiveness of downward communication," one writer states, "is directly correlated to how good upward communications are. . . . Leaders encouraging subordinates to communicate freely with them tend to have their downward communications accepted much more readily."[5] When a boss solicits or welcomes his subordinates' ideas, they are more likely to feel sympathetic with and take a greater interest in *his* views and problems. Furthermore, a superior's willingness to listen may serve as a psychological outlet for subordinates' suppressed emotional problems, which otherwise might seriously hamper their performance and the effectiveness of his downward communication.

Trust, deemphasis of status barriers, and receptiveness to two-way communication help create a favorable climate for communication, but it is primarily up to the *manager* to establish such an environment. The inherent barriers to communication that exist because of the manager's rank must be minimized, and that must be done by the manager himself. Of course, some organizational factors may be beyond his control and seriously hamper his setting the proper communication environment. Low pay, poor working conditions, or a boss who does not allow him to represent workers' legitimate grievances may seriously restrict an individual manager's control over the communication environment in his department.

CONSIDER THE OBJECTIVES OF YOUR COMMUNICATION

Most of a manager's interpersonal contacts occur without much warning and may not allow much preplanning. Yet he can anticipate many communication situations and give thought to them *before* they occur. Examples are when he has to tell subordinates their performance evaluation, discipline them and make work corrections, delegate authority for a job and communicate job assignments and instructions, persuade them to accept changes in the job or work environment, and when he has to persuasively communicate with a superior or other staff members interpersonally or at group meetings.

A manager must know how communication works so that he can formulate a communications plan. By understanding the complexity involved in communicating accurately, a manager can be more aware of barriers and try to minimize their effects. Moreover, for understanding to occur among himself and his subordinates, he must put himself in his subordinates' shoes, zero in on their patterns of evaluation, and consider other factors such as timing or selection of proper environment.

Once a manager establishes an objective for a communication, he then makes a plan to achieve it. Suppose, for instance, a subordinate has asked in advance to speak to his superior about a transfer to another department. The superior's objective, then, is to gain insight into the nature of the transfer, the reasons for it, and other facts so that he can make a decision or make readjustments in the department. His plan would be to take on a listening role, using techniques of nondirective interviewing (a listening-oriented role used by psychotherapists and counselors, which we will explain more in the next chapter). This strategy prevents the superior from taking command of the interaction, monopolizing communication and preventing completion of the objective.

In another example, if a promising subordinate is to be asked to participate in a voluntary training program for middle management, then the superior's objective is to gain the subordinate's acceptance of the program and develop enthusiasm for his participation. The manager's plan, then, is to focus on the benefits to the subordinate of participation in the program, to gear his message toward his subordinate's self-interest and needs, to show him how training would aid his development, his future potential in the company, and so on. The manager would try to uncover any objections, using nondirective interviewing and listening skills, and would attempt to anticipate possible objections in advance and determine how they could be overcome.

These two examples illustrate the advantage of a precommunication plan. If a manager fails to plan when he can do so, it means he is placing a great deal of dependence upon his spontaneous, off-the-cuff ability to communicate.

The planning stage of communication, therefore, spills over into the act of communication itself. The nature of the manager's communication role, the message(s), and strategy in message content and sequence can to some extent be predetermined. Thus, the four major concepts presented in the rest of the chapter relate to planning.

BE SENSITIVE TO YOUR SUBORDINATE'S PATTERNS OF EVALUATION

We have mentioned that a manager should be sensitive to his subordinate's frame of reference. Let us now examine some of the difficulties and limitations.

Perhaps the major barrier to a manager's ability to empathize or put himself in his subordinate's shoes is the tendency to stereotype his subordinates. To overcome this tendency, a manager should consider these questions: In what way is this subordinate like myself? In what way is he different? How is he similar to other subordinates? Different from them?[6]

Engage in Two-Way Communication

The best way to gain sensitivity to another individual is by plain old two-way communication; through it, a manager can learn to understand his subordinates—their reactions to job changes, their most important motivations and needs, their responsiveness to leadership styles, and so on. But as his span of management increases, more empathic ability is required. A large span of management results in fewer job contacts, which in turn makes it more difficult for the manager to accurately predict his subordinates' individual feelings and sensitivities.

Use Empathy

Empathy improves a superior's ability to interpret the messages his subordinates send. Psychotherapist Carl Rogers says the major gateway to improved communication is the ability to empathize while listening: "It [empathy] means to see the expressed idea and attitude from the other person's view, to sense how it feels to him, to achieve his frame of reference in regarding to the thing he is talking about."[7]

Consider, for example, the subordinate who is a "yes man," who consistently filters out unfavorable information when discussing his department's progress with superiors. The empathic manager understands the impact of his own status and authority, and may create many adjustments in his interpretation of this subordinate's message. Of course, the communication environment, as we discussed earlier, strongly determines the extent to which subordinates tend to filter out unfavorable information in their messages.

How to Develop Empathy

Gaining empathy is hard work. As one communications expert puts it, "It is a time-consuming operation continually to interpret the world from someone else's point of view . . . it is work to get to 'know' people."[8] Empathy depends on three factors being present: (1) As we mentioned, the superior must communicate with a limited number of subordinates. (2) The superior must be basically sensitive to human behavior. (3) The superior must recognize the value of communicating with his subordinates.

Managers differ greatly in their social sensitivity, in their ability to notice differences in the way subordinates feel and in how well they can predict subordinates' behavior. In summing up research findings on the characteristics of the empathic person, one author notes: "The most sensitive person is the most highly motivated, most open to new experience, and ready to participate in learning about others, and most able to assess the adequacy of what he has learned . . . sympathetic to new ideas about people. . . . The more curious, plastic, and nondefensive he is, the more likely he is to learn. The sensitive are more empirical, tolerant, liberal, and readier for change than the insensitive. . . . In sum, the most sensitive person is the one best equipped to learn about people. He is curious about, and deeply involved with others."[9]

The manager who sees a reward (better relations, more co-operation, stronger motivation, greater acceptance of change) in predicting subordinates' behavior—who recognizes the value of sensitivity, of knowing his subordinates' differences, individual needs, strengths, and weaknesses and can use this information advantageously—is, of course, more highly motivated to empathize.

IDENTIFY YOUR MESSAGE WITH YOUR SUBORDINATE'S SELF-INTEREST

A manager's primary duty is to guide his subordinates' behavior toward fulfilling specific organizational objectives, and if he is able to state his communications in terms of the benefits the subordinates will receive, his messages are more likely to be accepted by them. Situations in which the manager must be persuasive with subordinates are when he must gain their acceptance of a new job process or assignment; have them accept changes in job duties; change their attitudes toward work, work group members, or perhaps their role in the organization; have them accept the results of a performance appraisal. Let us look now at how communication may be used as a managerial tool in coping more effectively with various types of "persuasive" work situations.

Changing Subordinates' Attitudes

An attitude has been defined as someone's predisposition to evaluate something in a favorable or unfavorable manner.[10] A subordinate has attitudes toward his boss, his work, his fellow workers, the organization, and so on. Here we will discuss how the manager can make use of "persuasive" type messages to change attitudes. *i.e. predisposition*

Although change is a major characteristic of organizational life, a common individual and group reaction is resistance to change. We resist change because we see it as a threat to our present attitudes or ways of thinking or doing things. Frequently, changes required of people in organizations are presented only in terms of what management expects of them, with little or no attempt to gain acceptance. As two behavioral scientists point out, "To give up well-established and therefore easy habits, to spend time and acquire new knowledge, or to experience the possible threat of new conditions of work, all upset the even tenor of our adjustment. Unless there is more to be gained than lost and unless the gain is made apparent, we naturally resist having to change. Too often changes required of people in the organization are presented only as a management demand. When this happens, the individual fails to see any value in it for himself, there may be either a passive dragging of the feet, or a more active resistance to the change."[11]

Studies have shown that if a subordinate is allowed to actively participate in planning or carrying through a change, his resistance to it will be minimized. Besides using a participative approach (which is actually a management philosophy rather than a communication skill), a manager can use communication to smooth the way for change in three ways. First, he can use two-way communication to let his subordinate see that a change will *not* upset his equilibrium—not cause a status loss, loss of job security, and so on. Second, he can communicate details of the change, so that much of the uncertainty can be removed. Third, perhaps most important, he can let the subordinate see the changes as being compatible with his self-interest.

One research study showed that when people in an audience were forewarned of a speaker's attempt to change their opinion toward a subject, they changed their attitude less than when they were not forewarned about the speaker's intention.[12] By being prewarned, their defenses were aroused, thus preventing acceptance of the speaker's viewpoints. Similarly, in an organization, when inaccurate details of an impending change are transmitted through rumor or unofficial channels, employees develop built-in defenses over time, making it more difficult for a manager to gain acceptance of the change. Thus, if a manager communicates the nature of the planned change sufficiently early, his subordinates will not be able to develop unwarranted attitudes of resistance, and so acceptance of the change will be more likely.

A manager capable of empathizing should recognize the psychological undercurrents of resistance to change. He should see his job as one of minimizing anxiety, tension, or uncertainly in his subordinates. Even in situations where a participative leadership style is not feasible or workable, frank two-way communication may reduce the number of doubts and uncertainties and minimize the subordinates' resistance.

Determine Persuasive Message Strategy

Research studies point out that certain characteristics of persuasive messages most effectively bring about message acceptance. They may apply broadly to several situations where the manager's ability to communicate persuasively with subordinates is important. Here are eleven such characteristics.

1. A subordinate is more likely to respond to persuasive communication that is in line with his present attitudes, and to accept or resist accordingly. It follows that a manager will secure the most response in line with his intentions when the subordinate sees the message in a way that coincides with his present attitudes and feelings.

2. A persuasive message has a greater chance of success if a need is aroused first and then the information presented, rather than if the need arousal occurs after the information is presented.

3. At times it is better for the manager to state the cons as well as the pros of his particular persuasive message. Giving only one side of the story usually accomplishes more immediate acceptance, if the subordinate will not hear conflicting arguments from another source. However, if he *will* hear conflicting arguments, it is wise for the manager to state both sides initially. When the manager states both the advantages and disadvantages, his subordinate is more likely to consider him objective. Long run acceptance of his message is therefore more probable.

4. When a manager plans to mention both pro and con arguments, it is best to state the pro before the con.

5. It is often advantageous to state desired conclusions speci-

fically and positively. A message is more likely to be accepted if it is stated in positive terms (what can be done) rather than negative terms (what cannot be done).

6. When possible, the manager should provide his subordinate with access to another person who is favorable to the desired change. Needs should be aroused within the subordinate that will lead to his seeking out and using the information. For example, if a manager wants to persuade a subordinate to attend a one-week management training program, but does not want to command him to attend, he can say something like, "Bill, to help you see the value of this training, why don't you talk to Jim Roberts, who went last year?"

7. The manager should do everything possible to make the subordinate feel he had a choice. The subordinate tends to view the manager's opinions or attitudes with less defensiveness if he feels that he has *chosen* to behave in new ways and that these new ways have led to new opinions or attitudes.

8. When a subordinate's opinions do change because of a manager's communication, there is a tendency to return to the earlier position unless the new opinions are reinforced by events, other communications, or group influences. A subordinate who recently changes an opinion or attitude is likely to seek out supportive communications on the matter to reinforce his recent decision to change the attitude. So the manager potentially plays a major role in reinforcing desirable attitudes that have recently been formed.

9. Strong emotional appeals (fear, threat, and so on) often result in a greater immediate effect, but milder appeals seem to contribute to more long-run acceptance. The manager must therefore consider the urgency of the desired change, for if his subordinate's defensiveness is aroused, the manager's threats may backfire completely. Moreover, if the manager allows his subordinate to blow off steam and express his ideas and feelings, the subordinate may then see that the change is not a threat.

10. The more trustworthy, credible, or prestigious the manager appears to his subordinates, the more they will tend to accept his message.

11. The more attached a subordinate is to group norms and the more active his role as a group member, the more his group membership determines his response to individual face-to-face communication with the manager.

Communicate Job Assignments and Instructions Persuasively

A subordinate's compliance with his superior's job assignments and daily work orders may be automatic, but the manager should still communicate them effectively so that the subordinate will feel strongly committed to carrying out the instructions. Frequently, if a subordinate knows the background facts about an assignment, he will have greater incentive to complete the task. For example, if a manager gives his secretary background facts about a letter she is to type—such things as the personality of the party to receive the letter or the situation involved in the letter—the assignment thus takes on a more personal tone and the secretary probably devotes more attention to the assignment.

Allowing the subordinate to contribute his own ideas toward completing the assignment also adds to his motivation. Superiors can allow subordinate participation, which makes the subordinate feel a more active part of the assignment and strengthens his dedication toward completing the task effectively. Extensive studies have found that more effective supervisors tend to give general instructions, which allow subordinates to use their own initiative in filling out details.[14] And a study at General Electric on giving orders showed that least effective foremen gave three times as many authoritarian types of orders as did the most effective foremen.[15] The manager may also provide his subordinate with built-in motivation for an assignment by showing the importance of the assignment to him, the superior, the department, or the organization. To successfully identify a message with a subordinate's interests, we should recall, a manager must have some knowledge of the subordinate's interests, needs, and motives.

BE SENSITIVE TO THE LANGUAGE USED

All communication involves two major assumptions: (1) the sender assumes that the receiver interprets the message as the sender intended him to, and (2) the receiver assumes that he interprets the message as the sender intended it. But having to rely on word symbols in order to transfer meaning creates many opportunities for communications breakdowns. Suppose a superior hands his subordinate an important assignment, instructing him to "Get on it the first chance you have." By this, the superior means that the assignment should be completed within the next several hours. However, several hours later when the superior calls his subordinate and asks for the completed assignment, the subordinate replies, "I haven't gotten to it yet. I thought I'd get to it later this afternoon after getting out all of the regular work." The subordinate erroneously assumes that he had adequately captured the superior's intended meaning; the superior, unfortunately, did likewise.

Some writers believe message symbols are the most important part of communication, and so give prescriptions such as "Communicate clearly." But to treat message symbols apart from the sender and receiver of them clearly misrepresents the communication process. Understanding depends on whether the receiver's evaluation corresponds to the sender's meaning. Thus, the preoccupation with words themselves, apart from the frames of reference of the individuals involved, seems unjustified.

Even if an agreed-upon set of perfectly "clear" words could be established, such clarity should not necessarily be considered an end in itself. A "clear" message can be contradicted by a sender's nonverbal behavior and thus the effectiveness of the verbal symbols destroyed. If a manager verbally shows interest in a subordinate's job problems, but yawns several times during the discussion, his irritated subordinate may assign a higher priority to his boss's nonverbal than to his verbal cues. Thus, it is the parties involved in the communication, rather than the words chosen, that are the critical aspect of comunication.

Use Repetition

Message redundancy, or repetition, can play an important part in communicating effectively. This is especially true when a supervisor transmits technical information or a direct order. Redundancy reduces the risk of incorrect assumptions by the sender or receiver of a message. For example, a complicated message can be stated in several ways, and its intended meaning clarified by the use of examples, illustrations, or comparisons. The superior can specify in several ways the interpretation desired of the receiver.

Here, for instance, is how a manager might communicate an instruction to a subordinate: "Bill, we just got a telephone order

for a 42-by-36-inch firescreen in our KL-17 series. I know you
haven't done one up like it since last year, when that old gal gave
us so much trouble about the screen not fitting her fireplace
opening. That's the same style this guy wants, with black and gold
trim like this catalog clipping. And you heard me right, he wants it
42 inches high by 36 inches wide—higher than it is wide. That's
a new one on me, and I'm sure it's a new one for you. Can you get
it out in the next two weeks?"

Note how the supervisor used the past example and the
catalog to clarify the style of the firescreen and also how he reinforced the measurements.

Be Aware of Connotative Meaning

Interaction with subordinates provides a manager with the only
real opportunity to recognize the different ways they may interpret
the messages he sends. As we pointed out earlier, there may be
broad differences in managers' and subordinates' perceptions of
certain terms such as *quota, conference,* or *performance appraisal.*
Since it is impossible to eliminate differences in frames of reference, a more practical approach is to recognize the differences
in evaluation and to account for them when we send and receive
messages. A manager must ask himself, "Am I saying this in a way
that is acceptable to my listener? What is his reaction going to be
to this—how will he probably take my message?" Thus, being
sensitive to individual differences is a main step for a manager
toward clearer, more understandable messages.

Although we have devoted little space in this chapter to
language or symbols, it does not mean that symbols are not crucial
to communication accuracy. Actually, in much of the chapter—
especially the section on empathy and sensitivity to individual
differences—we emphasized the importance in choice of symbols,
verbal or otherwise. We feel that the manager who understands
the assumptions involved in communication takes a strong positive
step to make his messages better understood by subordinates.

USE FEEDBACK

Two ways a manager can use feedback to communicate better with
his subordinates are, first, he can create an environment where

feedback is encouraged and, second, he can induce feedback by his own action. We already discussed, at the beginning of the chapter, the importance of establishing a favorable climate for communication, and this certainly pertains to feedback. A subordinate should not be looked down on for asking questions or for openly stating his opinions, suggestions, or feelings toward a subject; a defensive attitude by the superior discourages feedback by subordinates. How the manager communicates also determines, to a large extent, the amount of feedback he receives. Written instructions or memos, for example, do not allow the immediate feedback found in oral, face-to-face communication.

Although the type of communication used and the communication environment are important in determining what feedback exists, a superior's responsibility for generating feedback goes beyond these factors; he must take an active role in inducing a response from his receiver. For example, after communicating a job assignment, a manager might ask "Do you have any questions?" or "Did I leave anything out?" But a more direct phrase would be "To make sure I've gotten my message across, how about repeating the process to me?" Frequently this produces a number of clarifications that a subordinate might otherwise be unwilling to mention for fear of looking stupid. Finally, the superior can set the stage for further feedback by comments such as "If anything comes up later, or you have some questions, just let me know."

Essentially, participative management consists of two-way communication, a form of feedback. When a superior allows his subordinates to make decisions or express opinions, their responses are a form of feedback which helps the superior better understand his subordinates' thinking.

However simple the feedback principle may appear, we often too readily assume that our messages are effectively received by others. Moreover, no-feedback situations or an unfavorable feedback climate often are simply to protect some manager's egos, since message inaccuracy goes unnoticed. The tendency to dispense with feedback is present in each of us and probably increases to the extent that we find ourselves in positions of power.[16] Higher level managers may therefore have a stronger tendency than others to practice one-way communication.

Feedback in communication also serves as a learning instrument for framing future messages. When a manager learns that his initial message was not clear, or his persuasiveness was less than effective, he can learn a valuable lesson to help him refine his future messages.

SUMMARY

There are six steps that will help a manager communicate with his subordinates. (1) He can establish the proper communication climate within his department so that his subordinates will be motivated to level with him in communicating more accurately their true feelings, attitudes, and problems. (2) He can carefully consider his objectives before communicating with subordinates and derive communication plans. (3) He can be sensitive to his subordinates' needs, interests, and frames of reference in adapting his messages to them. (4) He can arrange his messages so that they will most likely be consistent with subordinates' self-interests, thus increasing the probability that they will be well accepted. (5) He can develop a sensitivity to the fact that words take on different meanings, depending on the situation and the personalities and backgrounds of the parties involved. (6) He can encourage and induce feedback from subordinates so that understanding is maximized.

QUESTIONS

1. Discuss the following. A manager says "I've got a problem with these workers and I don't understand what to do. I'll go over a job, carefully explaining what should be done. I use examples, and try to make it as easy as possible. When I ask if anybody has questions, they seldom do. So I naturally assume they know what I'm talking about. But then, half the time they'll go out and mess up the job. I just don't know what to do."
2. In what way is a manager's "open door" policy helpful in stimulating upward communication by his subordinates? What are its limitations?
3. Of the six concepts presented in this chapter, which do you think is the single most important one, and why? Prepare your case carefully.
4. Think of some personal situations where having a communications plan in advance of the actual situation would prove helpful.
5. What are some practical difficulties in "putting yourself in the other fellow's shoes" when we try to understand his feeling and frame of reference?

NOTES

1. Harold P. Zelko and Harold J. O'Brien, *Management-Employee Communication in Action* (Cleveland, Ohio: Howard Allen, 1957), p. 40

2. Morton Deutsch, "Cooperation and Trust: Some Theoretical Notes," in Warren Bennis, Edgar Schein, Fred Steele, and David Berlew, eds., *Interpersonal Dynamics: Essays and Readings in Human Interaction* (Homewood, Ill.: Dorsey Press, 1964), p. 569.

3. Rensis Likert, *New Patterns of Management* (New York: McGraw-Hill Book Company, 1961), pp. 119–34.

4. George Homans, *The Human Group* (New York: Harcourt Brace Jovanovich, 1950), p. 438.

5. S. G. Huneryager, "Essentials of Effective Leadership," *Supervision*, May, 1963, p. 5.

6. Robert Tannenbaum, Irwing Weschler, and Fred Massarik, *Leadership and Organization* (New York: McGraw-Hill Book Company, 1961), p. 738.

7. Carl Rogers and F. J. Roethlisberger, "Barriers and Gateways to Communication," in George Sanborn and W. Charles Redding, eds., *Business and Industrial Communication: A Source Book* (New York: Harper & Row, 1964), p. 5.

8. David Berlo, *The Process of Communication* (New York: Holt, Rinehart and Winston, 1960), p. 134.

9. Henry Smith, *Sensitivity to People* (New York: McGraw-Hill Book Company, 1966), pp. 176–79.

10. Daniel Katz, "The Functional Approach to the Study of Attitudes," in Costello and Zalkind, *Psychology in Administration*, p. 251.

11. Timothy Costello and Sheldon Zalkind, *Psychology in Administration* (Englewood Cliffs, N.J.: Prentice-Hall, 1963), p. 227.

12. Leon Festinger and Jane Allyn, "The Effectiveness of Unanticipated Persuasive Communication," *Journal of Abnormal and Social Psychology*, May, 1961, pp. 35–40.

13. See Wilbur Schramm, ed., *The Process and Effects of Mass Communication* (Urbana, Ill.: University of Illinois Press, 1954), pp. 296–97; B. Berelson and C. Steiner, *Human Behavior: An Inventory of Scientific Findings* (New York: Harcourt Brace Jovanovich, 1964), pp. 529–41; Costello and Zalkind, *Psychology in Administration*, pp. 296–97; Carl Hovland, ed., *The Order of Presentation in Persuasion* (New Haven, Conn.: Yale University Press, 1957), pp. 130–37.

14. Saul Gellerman, *Motivation and Productivity* (New York: American Management Association, 1963), pp. 32–36; also George Strauss and Leonard Sayles, *Personnel: The Human Problems of Management*, rev. ed. (Englewood Cliffs, N.J.: Prentice-Hall, 1967), pp. 143–73.

15. Willard V. Merrihue, *Managing by Communication* (New York: McGraw-Hill Book Company, 1960), p. 119.

16. Peter Nokes, "Feedback As an Explanatory Device in the Study of Certain Interpersonal and Institutional Processes," *Human Relations*, November, 1961, p. 384.

9

Interviewing and Appraisal:
Handling the Human Problems

As a manager you may have to listen to remarks like these: "I just can't seem to get fired up about my job anymore; I think I need a transfer." "I guess you called me in to ask why my work has been so poor recently. I knew I had it coming." "Listen, that young personnel manager had better keep his nose out of my department. Some of the men have been losing work time because of his little visits, and I'm going to have to tell him where to get off."

Every manager must spend some time dealing with such human problems, and this chapter shows you how to use interviewing skills to handle them. It also focuses on the performance appraisal and the performance-appraisal interview—parts of the job that many managers dread.

TWO KINDS OF INTERVIEWING:
DIRECTIVE AND NONDIRECTIVE

In the two preceding chapters, we pointed out the barriers a manager must overcome to effectively communicate and what he can do to minimize them. Obviously, the better he understands his subordinates' frames of reference, the better he is able to interpret their behavior and to adapt his own behavior toward them. Since interviewing is a communication process, the principles of communication we discussed also apply generally to interviewing.

There are essentially two approaches to interviewing—directive and nondirective. Each has its own merits, depending on the situation. The *directive* interview is led by the interviewer; before the interview begins, he has a good idea of the subject to be followed, what he will say, and what specific information he will try to obtain from the interviewee. A directive approach is most commonly used in orienting new workers, in training, and in giving job instructions.

The *nondirective* interview focuses on the interviewee himself.[1] Instead of making a prescribed list of statements or questions, the interviewer tries to let the interviewee himself control the progress of the interview. Nondirective interviewing places the interviewer in the role of a highly perceptive listener whose job is to encourage the interviewee to express his inner feelings and attitudes. Thus, the interviewer seeks to understand the interviewee's frame of reference. The nondirective approach can be used by a manager in any number of situations: counseling subordinates, discussing job problems, communicating results of performance appraisals, correcting poor performance, and so on.

The Nondirective Interview: How It Works

Our emphasis in this chapter is on the nondirective approach because of its broad application. The manager who can understand the nondirective approach and use it effectively can definitely add a new dimension to his management skills. Let us, then, take a look at how this kind of interview works. Consider the following interchange between a plant superintendent and one of his production foremen.

FOREMAN: You wanted to see me, Jim?
SUPERINTENDENT: Yes, I did. I'll be right with you, have a seat. [*He talks on the phone for about four minutes, his tone of voice showing that he is upset about something, then hangs up.*] Bill, to get right to the point, I just checked with Quality Inspection, and the situation on those rejects coming out of

your department is really getting intolerable. What's going on? I've never seen anything like it.

FOREMAN [*fidgeting*]: Well, Jim, I think it's mostly these new people I got last week during the rush. I talked with them about it, for whatever good that'll do.

SUPERINTENDENT: They can't cut it, huh? So what am I supposed to do? You want me to put an inspector directly in your department? The other departments got a lot of new people in the last few weeks, too, but they don't seem to be having problems. Bill, it's your job to get quality work from these men, you know that!

FOREMAN: Well, of course usually there'd be no trouble, but these guys got only one week's training instead of two. I help them when I can, naturally, but I've got twenty others to worry about, too, you know.

SUPERINTENDENT: I think one week is probably time enough, and anyway these reject errors are things almost anybody would probably catch, even with one day's training.

FOREMAN: Well, I only want to say . . .

SUPERINTENDENT [*Interrupting*]: Look, this big rush with three shifts has caused us all some problems, Bill . . . [*Phone rings.*] Excuse me. Anderson speaking. Yes, sir, I'll bring the reports right up. [*To Foreman.*] I've got to go upstairs a second. I know you can straighten this thing out. [*Rises and walks over to Foreman, who rises also, and both start toward the door.*] I told Quality Inspection to get the information to you more quickly when bad units come up, and I know you'll take care of this matter. Listen, neither one of us likes to have to talk about this, but you know we just can't operate this way at this time of year. Okay, if I can do anything to help, let me know. [*Pats Foreman on shoulder, and both turn and walk away.*]

Is this interaction typical? Unfortunately, it is. The superintendent is too busy to listen and indeed has a poor attitude toward listening to begin with. He seems to tell the foreman, "Don't tell me any more facts; I know them already."

What about the foreman? Perhaps the problem will eventually get solved in his department, but if his boss had used good nondirective interviewing techniques, the foreman would have felt freer to discuss his problem, to feel that his boss was open-minded and was concerned for his views and feelings; there would have been stronger rapport between the two men.

Did Bill have some suggestions about possible changes in training techniques? Or does he feel inspection points in the manufacturing process could be changed? Does he think he's been receiving more than his share of ill-trained workers? Is he thinking of quitting? What does he think is the best solution to his present problem? Obviously, the superior passed up an opportunity both to gain helpful information and to gain the foreman's respect for his fairness and sensitivity.

The Rules of Nondirective Interviewing

Nondirective interviewing in industry was first used during the two-year Hawthorne studies in the late 1920s at Western Electric.[2] So favorably impressed were Western Electric officials with this interviewing program that in 1936 they employed some "personnel counselors," whose main job was simply to listen to employees' problems.

In 1928 the original Hawthorne interviewers had done this as part of their initial interviewing. At first, they had asked a number of direct questions about the workers' jobs but found that many answers were irrelevant or too brief. Eventually, instead of asking questions, they encouraged employees to talk about anything that concerned them.

This new program established several important rules for conducting interviews, and they remain the core of nondirective interviewing today:

1. The interviewer should listen to the speaker in a patient and friendly, but intelligently critical, manner.
2. The interviewer should not display any kind of authority.
3. The interviewer should not give advice or moral admonition.
4. The interviewer should not argue with the speaker.
5. The interviewer should talk or ask questions only under certain conditions:
   a. To help the person talk.

  b. To relieve any fears or anxieties on the part of the speaker which may be affecting his relation to the interviewer.

  c. To praise the interviewee for reporting his thoughts and feelings accurately.

  d. To veer the discussion to some topic which has been omitted or neglected.

  e. To discuss implicit assumptions, if this is advisable.[3]

Let us examine how you can use each rule, keeping in mind that nondirective interviewing should enable the person interviewed to talk in an open manner about his feelings and attitudes.

Listen in a Friendly, Patient Manner. The quickest way to stop someone from expressing himself is to interrupt. Remember that the interviewee may have difficulty stating what is important to him. Besides actively listening and not interrupting, show a sincere interest in what he says and try to understand it.

Do Not Display Authority or Status. Make the interviewee feel at ease and encourage him to discuss his feelings. Because he will probably resent and become defensive at any display of authority, do not do such things as contradict him, interrupt him, take the role of teacher, or treat his ideas lightly.

Do Not Give Advice or Make Moral Judgments. If the interviewee says "This is a terrible place to work, and the work assignments are awful," do not say, "Sorry about that, but your attitude isn't the greatest either." Do not cut him off or dismiss him lightly. Instead, give him a chance to express himself. Ask him "Why do you feel this way?" or say "Tell me more about this." He can then discuss his feelings more deeply without becoming defensive.

Do Not Argue. If you argue with the interviewee, it only makes him defensive and prevents him from revealing his true feelings. The best way to avoid arguing is to try to become psychologically detached from your own opinions, beliefs, and feelings. If, for example, the interviewee criticizes you directly (or indirectly), be ready to ask, "Why do you feel this way?"

Talk or Ask Questions Sparingly.   Perhaps the most useful rule for nondirective interviewing is this: You should speak out or ask questions only under five conditions.

1. To encourage the interviewee to talk freely about himself, his job, or problems, using comments such as "Isn't that interesting?", "Really!", "What do you mean?", "Tell me more about it."

2. To relieve any fears the interviewee may have that may affect his relation with you. A person may be reluctant to discuss job-related or personal problems, and you may assure him that what he says will be held in confidence and urge him to be frank in discussing his feelings.

3. To praise the interviewee for accurately reporting his thoughts and feelings, using comments such as, "Well, I appreciate your giving it to me straight and your willingness to discuss the problem."

4. To steer the discussion to some topic that has been omitted or only briefly mentioned. This is easiest when the interviewee has begun expressing himself freely and has greater confidence in your willingness to listen.

5. To discuss assumptions underlying the conversation that have not been expressed. It is frequently helpful in stimulating the discussion to bring out such an assumption directly. If one worker has been discussing his inability to work with another worker and throughout the interview has been calling him a college-know-it-all with all the answers, you might say, "What you seem to be saying is that you would not like to work with anyone who has been through college, is that it?" He may welcome hearing you state this assumption and then discuss the matter deeply. (At other times, stating such an assumption may embarrass the interviewee and discourage his openness, so obviously some judgment is called for.)

How a Manager May Use Nondirective Interviewing

During World War II several industrial firms followed Western Electric in employing personnel counselors to listen to workers' problems, but later the use of these counselors diminished—one 1958 study showed that less than 20 percent of the firms surveyed employed a specialized counselor.[4]

At least three drawbacks to such counseling were that (1)

though counseling might help a worker adjust better to his problem, it could seldom do anything about the problem itself; (2) it was expensive to hire such specialists; (3) the role of the supervisor tended to be ignored.[5] Actually, the supervisor is often best able to help someone adjust to working conditions, style of supervision, or work load and assignments, since he often directly controls these factors. Furthermore, because the worker's problems often affect his work performance, attendance, and relationships on the job, his supervisor has an immediate concern in these matters. Thus, today the tendency is to emphasize the role of the supervisor as a counselor and to educate him in the use of nondirective interviewing techniques. Since he knows his subordinates better than a staff specialist would, he should be better able to listen to their problems, although he should recognize his limitations where their problems are particularly acute and be willing to refer them to trained specialists.

The typical manager can use the nondirective approach as a problem-solving tool. By encouraging his subordinates to discuss their problems and showing his willingness to listen, he will be better able to understand their needs, motivations, attitudes, and feelings about their jobs. His listening will serve as a valuable form of upward communications. But merely listening may not satisfy subordinates' expectations that their superior should help them solve their problems. How can the nondirective interviewing approach be used for problem solving?

In the directive approach, the manager provides the subordinate with the answers to solving the problem. In the nondirective approach, the subordinate, after discussing his problem with his superior and coming to see it more clearly, solves his own problem. The theory is that the interviewee will most likely be committed to changing his behavior to cope with a problem when he himself originates and accepts the change as being best. This is much different from the relatively easy task of the manager's listening to a worker's problems and then saying "Now here's what you ought to do," for this assumes the superior knows more about the subordinate's problem than the subordinate does—a fact that is frequently untrue. Moreover, such advice giving may also backfire, since it provides the subordinate with a ready-made excuse if the advice proves wrong.

How can the manager avoid playing advice giver and still help the subordinate solve his problem? In the nondirective approach, he could respond by saying, "Bill, what do you see as some alternatives for dealing with this problem?" or, "What would probably happen if you went along with the first alternative you mentioned?" Obviously, the manager can help clarify the subordinate's thinking about his own problem, yet refrain from directly giving advice.

Even after listening to a subordinate's problem, and encouraging him to discuss and consider various alternatives, the superior may have several alternatives or suggestions that might prove helpful. Should he avoid mentioning them because the subordinate has not thought of them? Certainly not. But he should avoid saying "Here is what you ought to do," or "Here's what I would do in your place." He can simply say "You've mentioned several alternatives, and we've discussed them. How do you think such and such would work out?" or "Have you considered the possibility of . . . ?" In this way the interviewer is not placed in the position of having to defend and support a suggestion, but he still was able to have the subordinate consider it.

Three Tools of Nondirective Interviewing

The Reflective Statement. The reflective statement[6] basically works like this. A worker tells his boss, "Say, I've got a little problem I'd like to discuss. It's about Klaric, the new man in my department. He doesn't seem to fit in at all. Some of my men have even kidded me about it—you know, 'Where did you dig this guy up?' He's a real weirdo; he won't even try to fit in, and the others seem to resent him for that. I've tried to help him work into the group, because you know the pride my guys have in their work and in getting along so well together. Klaric's an excellent worker, but he's causing me more trouble than he's worth."

What is the subordinate telling his superior? How would you respond to him? One way is to respond in your own words with a summary of what your subordinate just told you: "So what you seem to be saying is that while Klaric is a good worker, you're concerned because he doesn't fit in well with the others." This statement reflects back to the interviewee what he has just said and allows him to continue talking about the subject.

Frequently, he will elaborate on certain aspects of the earlier statement which seem to him to be more critical. For example, he might respond by saying "Well, the thing that gets me most, I guess, is that I really messed up in my evaluation about Klaric. I honestly thought the guy *would* fit in. In fact, this was more important to me than his ability. I just don't see how I could have been so wrong in evaluating him." Thus, in elaborating on the more general statement of his problem, the interviewee has added a deeper dimension: we find he is mainly concerned about making a poor evaluation on Klaric's ability to fit into the department.

The Probe. This device is more specific than the reflective statement. The probe directs attention to a more specific aspect of what the interviewee has said. For example, in the Klaric case, the supervisor's response could have been any of the following: "Some of your men have been kidding you?" "You say the other men seem to resent him?" "He's a real weirdo, hey?" Note that these probes are more specific than the reflective statement, but they allow the supervisor to pursue an avenue of discussion he feels may be important, and may provide additional insight into the problem by encouraging the interviewee to discuss it more deeply. Also, a probe is less likely to cause defensiveness than direct questions such as "Who's been kidding you about it?" "Why do they seem to resent him?" "Why do you call him a weirdo?" Even when the supervisor feels a need for asking direct questions about matters that the worker has not yet brought out, but which the supervisor would like to know, he will have better success by delaying such questions until later stages of the interview.

The Pause. Occasionally the use of pauses also help the interviewee express himself. Essentially, a pause signals that one party has expressed himself and is awaiting a reply. After the interviewee has just completed a statement and pauses to await a reply, if the interviewer simply waits out the pause, the interviewee will often resume talking. Or during a pause, the interviewer can say "Uh-huh," "I see," or "I understand," to encourage the interviewee to continue talking.

A Philosophy of Interacting With People

Nondirective interviewing is more than a management tool; it is a philosophy of interacting with others. We have discussed it primarily from the standpoint of counseling workers, but it can still be a daily part of the manager's listening behavior. After all, listening is the process of trying to understand someone else's viewpoint. And reflective statements, probes, and other means of encouraging someone to further express his views apply broadly to all interactions with others.

The manager who uses the nondirective approach, however, must be willing to pay a price for the benefits he gains. First, the nondirective approach is time consuming. Second, by encouraging his subordinates to "open up," he may find himself in the occasionally uncomfortable position of hearing things that may discomfort or embarrass him or place him in a disturbing ethical position. When a subordinate seems likely to disclose something in confidence that the superior feels he cannot treat confidentially, he might forewarn the subordinate of that fact.

One final point is that there are many fine degrees between the direct and the nondirect approaches to interviewing. On a given occasion, the approach a manager may use will fall somewhere between the two. For example, a disciplinary interview may require that the superior gain certain specific facts from the subordinate, so a direct approach may be used initially. A shift may then be made in the direction of the nondirective approach as the superior attempts to learn more deeply about the subordinate's feelings. Or even in what is basically a nondirective interview, the subordinate may from time to time request certain job-related information from his superior. Moreover, where the superior has information that can help clarify certain points in the interview and help the subordinate's thinking, he should certainly present them.

Reading about interviewing in a book is no substitute for actual experience. We have presented the major points of the nondirective approach, and urge you to practice these principles daily, with friends, associates, and family. For good listening is a human, rather than a managerial skill. And there is little question that the manager who possesses skill in this basic listening tool will be a more effective manager.

APPRAISAL: NEW WAYS OF EVALUATING SUBORDINATES' WORK

In recent years, the traditional approach to evaluating the work of subordinates has been replaced by a concept variously known as *joint target-setting, management by objectives, appraisal by results,* and other names.[7] Just as the teacher uses tests, or the football coach studies films of the previous game and grades each player's performance, the business organization also has a need to measure the performance of its members. The newer approaches to appraisal involve the planning and controlling functions discussed in Chapter 3. As you will see, however, these new approaches also form an important part of participative management. Let us first examine briefly some of the traditional approaches organizations have used in evaluating performance.

The Traditional Methods of Performance Appraisal

Rating Scale. The oldest and most prevalent type of performance-rating procedure is the rating scale.[8] Every six or twelve months, the employee is rated on a number of characteristics: quality of work, attitude toward work, ability to get along with others, judgment, and other characteristics believed important by the organization. Each characteristic may be rated on a point scale ranging from 5 for "exceptional" down to 1 for "very poor." The points are totaled and the results used to compare subordinates' performances and point out needed areas of improvement. (An example of one type of rating scale is presented in Figure 20.)

The major advantage of this system is its simplicity, but several disadvantages are evident. An 85 score for one employee does not mean that he is more effective in his job than the man who receives an 83. Moreover, different supervisors may have different standards in mind for "above average" or "below average" work. In addition, supervisors may tend to rate their men high because it makes themselves look good, or because they honestly feel that their men are "above average."

Employee-Comparison Methods. To overcome the disadvantages of the rating scale, various employee-comparison methods are used. These differ from the rating system in that supervisors are required to rank each of their men in comparison to others as to performance and value to the organization. Thus, someone must end up being first, another second, and so on, down to the last. A variant of this approach is to select, say, the top third, the middle third, and the bottom third. Another variant is the *paired-comparison technique:* if a supervisor has five subordinates (Jones, Watkins, Smith, Harrison, Willard) and wants to evaluate Jones,

EMPLOYEE EVALUATION FORM

Employee Name *Fred Willis* Position *Chief Engineer, Materials Research*

Period covered by evaluation: from *6/1* to *7/1/75*.

	Unsatis-factory (1)	Meets minimum (2)	Average (3)	Above Average (4)	Out-standing (5)	Score
1. Quality and thoroughness of work		✓				2
2. Volume of work				✓		4
3. Knowledge of job, methods, and procedures				✓		4
4. Initiative and resourcefulness				✓		4
5. Cooperation, attitude, and team-work			✓			3
6. Adaptability and ability to learn quickly					✓	5
7. Ability to express self clearly in speaking and writing			✓			3
8. Planning, organizing, and making work assignments		✓				2
9. Selection and development of subordinates		✓				2
10. Morale and loyalty of subordinates			✓			3

Total score 32

What steps can this employee take to improve his work?

Employee is an eager, innovative, resourceful person whose eagerness sometimes causes him to sacrifice quality of work. While highly talented, must learn to delegate more technical work to subordinates and assume more managerial tasks himself.

Other comments:

Employee has been in position about 7 months. This is his first managerial job, and some problems in making the adjustment were expected.

Total score:
10-15   Unsatisfactory   Supervisor's signature *Paul Batson*
16-25   Meets minimum   Title *Head, Engineering Research*
26-35   Average   Employee's signature *Frederick R. Willis*
36-45   Above average   Approved by *Harold Wilhelm*
46-50   Outstanding   Title *Director, Research + Development*

Figure 20. Traditional employee appraisal form.

he will compare Jones and Watkins, Jones and Smith, Jones and Harrison, and Jones and Willard. The process is repeated for comparing each subordinate with each other. The number of times one subordinate is preferred over another is recorded, and the result is an overall ranking as to who received the most votes, next most votes, and so on. This technique is probably more scientific than the other comparison methods above, but it is more difficult when the superior has a larger number of subordinates.

Other Methods. There are a variety of other approaches to performance appraisal, most of them aimed at attaining greater objectivity in the evaluation. *Peer ratings* are sometimes used to have fellow workers evaluate the performance of people in their own ranks. Also, *subordinate ratings*, where subordinates rate their supervisor, have been introduced in a number of firms.[9] Still other firms may conduct *group appraisals* by having a committee or conference of two or more of the employee's superiors.

The Post-Appraisal Interview

Performance appraisals are conducted in most firms at regular intervals of every six months, or every year. Among the major purposes for appraisals are: wage and salary determination, promotion, training and development, helping workers know their progress, helping supervisors know their employees, and improving job performance. Typically, organizations require that supervisors communicate the results of performance appraisal to their subordinates. This seems most compatible with accomplishing feedback as to workers' progress and subsequent improvement on the job. However, it is this post-appraisal interview that has been criticized heavily as a relationship damaging factor between superior and subordinate.

The appraisal interview used to be along the line of "Call the man in, tell him what he has to straighten out and what's expected of him." Now, however, interviewers are expected to aim at cooperation, construction, and greater understanding. Most experts recommend use of nondirective-interviewing techniques in conducting appraisal interviews. But let us look at what tends to happen during the typical interview, even though it is conducted according to the rules of good performance-appraisal interviewing:

Usually on an annual basis the boss calls his employees into his office one at a time for the appraisal interview. Both parties tend to build up emotionally for this. The boss plans what he is going to say, and the subordinate tends to be apprehensive about what he is going to hear. When the actual interview commences, the supervisor tries to put the man at ease by talking about the weather, the latest big league ball game, his golf play, or his family. The employee knows that this is just an interlude before getting down to serious business. Then the supervisor explains his overall evaluation in broad terms. He initially mentions some good aspects of the employee's performance. He may then give the employee a chance to express his views. Next the supervisor tells him his weaknesses and past failures. He allows the man to explain himself. Then the supervisor explains what steps he must take to improve performance. He may, at this point, ask for the employee's ideas on improvement. One variation of this procedure above provides an opportunity, before the boss announces his evaluation, for the man to tell how he would rate himself.[10]

This conventional approach to the performance-appraisal interview is obviously an emotional experience for both superior and subordinate. There is no doubt that in the subordinate's mind, he is on the hot seat, and that there is no point disagreeing with his superior about his judgments. He has fast learned that it is best to simply remain submissive and accept the criticism, even if he disagrees with it.

Superiors likewise tend to feel anxiety over performance appraisal. As management theorist Douglas McGregor points out: "Managers are uncomfortable when they are put in the position of 'playing God.' The respect we hold for the inherent value of the individual leaves us distressed when we must take responsibility for judging the personal worth of a fellow man. Yet the conventional approach to performance appraisal forces us, not only to make such judgments and to see them acted upon, but also to communicate them to those we have judged. Small wonder we resist."[11]

The authors have talked with numerous managers who suffer the double-barreled discomforts of performance appraisal. They dislike being evaluated by their own bosses; they dislike evaluating their subordinates—or at least telling them the results. In one company, when supervisors were required to tell their appraisals to their subordinates, their evaluations of subordinates suddenly jumped remarkably.[12]

No doubt use of nondirective interviewing techniques can help a manager in the post-appraisal interview with his subordinate, but even these may not be enough. The fact that a superior makes judgments over his subordinate and communicates them often makes the subordinate so defensive that even good nondirective counseling techniques have little effect. Moreover, good counseling is definitely an art and does not come naturally to many of us.

Joint Target-Setting/Appraisal by Results

The criticisms above have given rise to a new technique of appraising which focuses on the employee's performance rather than his characteristics. The superior becomes less a judge than a helper.

Joint target-setting involves four steps.[13] First, superior and subordinate meet together and agree on the subordinate's job objectives and major responsibilities. The superior attempts to fit these into the overall broader objectives of his own job.

Second, both jointly agree on short-term goals or targets which the subordinate feels should be accomplished within the time period.

Third, periodically the subordinate reports his progress, problems, and developments to his superior, and sometimes they modify targets previously set. The superior also makes himself available as an aide on a day-to-day basis to help the subordinate accomplish his goals.

Fourth, at the end of the specified time period, they jointly appraise the results. To what extent were the targets reached? Which fell short and why? What personal growth and weaknesses did the subordinate feel in the time period in question? What most helped or hindered his growth on the job?

Under the appraisal-by-results technique, the role of judge has been removed from the superior. His main job is to help the subordinate grow and fit his aims into the broader objectives of the superior's responsibilities and ultimately those of the organization. The tone is positive rather than negative, constructive rather than destructive. The subordinate himself is heavily involved in his own evaluation and can feel on a weekly or even daily basis the extent of his development toward the targets that have been set. Thus, he should be in for no surprises at the final discussion with his superior, for each should have a good idea of how well the targets are being accomplished. The subordinate is actively involved in self-appraisal as he helps establish his goals, evaluates his strong and weak points, and periodically measures his progress.

Defining Quantifiable Targets

A target that is well defined has yardsticks along the way that can be used to measure progress. A poor statement of a target for example, would be "keep the department's absenteeism rate low." A more measurable goal would be "keep the absenteeism rate below 6 percent." Quantifiable targets can be set in production volume, quality standards, overtime, scrappage, cost control, turnover, and other areas. Obviously, the advantage of quantifiable targets is that they are objective and do not require so much personal judgment as to whether they were attained or not.

A goal must be meaningful to the man trying to accomplish it, and specific enough so he can measure whether he accomplished it. Of course, when goals are set, the superior should allow for factors over which his subordinate has no control. For example, if a sales manager sets up a target of a 10 percent sales increase, and his sales district suffers an unforeseen economic setback (such as the closing of a large areospace center), this must be accounted for in his final evaluation.

There is one danger in the use of quantifiable targets: if they are the *only* goals specified, a subordinate may tend to emphasize their accomplishment at the expense of others. The supervisor who strives to reach a target of X units of production may do so by extreme pressure on and overly close supervision of subordinates and so may seriously injure morale. Thus, though they may be more difficult to assess than quantifiable ones, "qualitative" targets are also important—"keeping subordinates better informed," for example, or "improving relations with the Personnel Department."

When qualitative targets are set, however, subordinate and superior should plan how to measure their accomplishment. The target of "keeping employees better informed," for instance, could be accomplished by the foreman's having a weekly departmental meeting or increasing the number of personal contacts on the job. Thus, though the overall target is "qualitative," the means of accomplishing the target can still be measured somewhat.

In joint target-setting, a manager must effectively use the nondirective concepts we discussed. For example in meeting to discuss targets, it is imperative that the supervisor allow the subordinate to discuss what he feels are appropriate targets and his reasons, for unless he can discuss his thinking and actually help influence the goal setting, the "jointness" in target setting will not be accomplished, and the advantage of the subordinate's involvement will be lost. Of course, the boss does not merely sit on the sidelines and accept targets set out by his subordinate. Frequently he has necessary information that will help in establishing suitable targets. Often the subordinate will set a target that the manager will think is unreasonably high or low. Thus, the resulting target is usually a compromise, with both parties giving in a bit.

Joint target-setting is a planning and controlling technique. Rather than being oriented toward the past it is forward looking. As a manager told one of the authors: "You know, if I had one major weakness as a manager it was that I didn't really plan things in my department. I just sort of took things on a day-to-day basis, you know. Then my boss comes at me with this JTS [joint target-setting] thing that he wants us to try out. Well, I felt pretty frustrated about it at first because I really couldn't see any set targets to have my department shoot for. It took a while for me to realize that my problem was that I just couldn't plan."

Since it involves a subordinate actively in the planning and control process, joint target-setting is a form of enlightened management. In Maslow's need hierarchy, it allows a subordinate to attain higher level needs. By feeling he has a part in guiding his own destiny, the subordinate tends to feel a greater sense of personal development and worth, and when his targets are attained, feels great satisfaction. Because it allows higher level need satisfaction and prevents superiors from playing the god role, this method will probably be even more widespread in the future.

However, joint target-setting does have some disadvantages. One is that it is time consuming—it requires several conferences between boss and subordinate. It is also not suitable for the worker level, where jobs are narower in scope and carefully defined. Their targets are already set by higher management, and the assembly-line worker whose job is to tighten a particular bolt in a fabrication process has little opportunity to set "targets."

Joint target-setting is also difficult to use for salary administration. Merit raises and promotions require consistent standards among departments and levels, and since joint target-setting results in different targets for different bosses and subordinates, it would be impractical to base merit raises solely on who accomplishes targets and who does not. Some subordinates may have higher goals than others. Some who do not meet their targets may have been affected by circumstances beyond their control. Because people are so sensitive about the subject of salary determination, salary discussions should be conducted in a different way.

SUMMARY

This chapter presented two subjects popular in management circles during the past few years. *Nondirective interviewing* can be used by all managers, and can add greatly to a manager's ability to gain insight into subordinates' feelings, attitudes, ideas, and problems, and help subordinates perform more efficiently on the job. Of the new approaches to *performance appraisal,* the joint target-setting/appraisal by results seems superior to traditional approaches. In this chapter, we have focused on superior-subordinate target setting. However, joint target-setting can also be a group process, where subordinates as a group work together with their superior in helping determine objectives and goals within their department. Traditionally, our management system has recognized the authority of the superior in determining his subordinates' objectives. It is uncomfortable for many managers to share this traditional "right" with their subordinates. However, "enlightened management" recognizes the manager's role as being more of a coach, helper, and aide than simply an authoritarian figure who calls all the plays himself and expects them to be carried out by highly motivated subordinates simply because he says so. We will probably find organizations making greater use of the joint target-setting/appraisal by results method in the future.

Whereas traditional approaches seem to rely mainly on a superior's subjective evaluation, joint target-setting/appraisal by results brings the subordinate into a self-evaluation and focuses on objective, quantifiable measurements. Superior and subordinate are both taken off the hot seat, and the boss's role becomes more that of a coach or helper.

QUESTIONS

1. What are the basic differences between the directive and the nondirective approaches to interviewing?
2. Discuss this manager's comments: "This nondirective interviewing is a bunch of malarky the psychologists dreamed up. When a man comes to you with a problem, he doesn't want a lot of fooling around, he wants you to tell him what to do. I've followed that rule for twenty years of management, and nobody who ever came to me with a problem has complained yet I didn't try to help them."
3. Suppose a subordinate tells you: "I really don't know what to do. My work has been slipping, I know. It's hard to get fired up on this packaging job anymore. I've been doing the same thing now for four years, and lately it's been boring me to death." Which response best depicts the nondirective approach and what effect would each response probably have on your subordinate?
   a. "Would you like to switch with Carlson and try his job out for awhile?"
   b. "Why don't you take a couple of days off and see if that helps?"
   c. "It's been boring you to death lately, huh?"
   d. "You're probably just a little tired because of the overtime we've been having. You'll snap out of it."
   e. "Have you been getting enough sleep?"
4. What are some reasons superiors and subordinates tend to resist performance-appraisal interviews?
5. How does joint target-setting/appraisal by results differ from traditional approaches to performance evaluation?
6. Suppose a company president becomes sold on joint target-setting/appraisal by results, and his company has never used this method before. What resistances might the president find in trying to have his line and staff managers use this approach with their subordinates?

NOTES

1. See Carl R. Rogers, *Counseling and Psychotherapy* (Boston: Houghton Mifflin, 1942) and *Client-Centered Therapy* (Boston: Houghton Mifflin, 1951). Also see Fritz Roethlisberger and W. J. Dickson, *Management and the Worker* (Cambridge, Mass.: Harvard University Press, 1939), pp. 189–205; 270–91.
2. Roethlisberger and Dickson, *Management and the Worker*, pp. 204–205.
3. *Ibid.*, p. 287.
4. Henry Eilbirt, "A Study on Counseling Practices in Industry," *Journal of Business*, January, 1958, pp. 28–37.
5. Dale Beach, *Personnel: The Management of People at Work* (New York: Macmillan Company, 1970), p. 545.

6. See Norman R. F. Maier, *Psychology in Industry*, 3rd ed. (Boston: Houghton Mifflin, 1965), pp. 655–63.

7. See Douglas McGregor, *The Human Side of Enterprise* (New York: McGraw-Hill Book Company, 1960), pp. 61–76; H. H. Meyer, E. Kay, and J. R. P. French, "Split Roles in Performance Appraisal," *Harvard Business Review*, January-February, 1965, pp. 123–29; Chester Harris and Reinald Heise, "Tasks, Not Traits—The Key to Better Performance," *Personnel*, May-June, 1964, pp. 60–64; and George Ordiorne, *Personnel Administration by Objectives* (Homewood, Ill.: Richard D. Irwin, 1971), pp. 108–24.

8. For an excellent discussion of the traditional approaches to performance appraisal, see George Strauss and Leonard Sayles, *Personnel: The Human Problems of Management*, rev. ed. (Englewood Cliffs, N.J.: Prentice-Hall, 1967), pp. 550–58, or Wendell French, *The Personnel Management Process*, 2nd ed. (Boston: Houghton Mifflin, 1970), pp. 291–310.

9. P. W. Maloney and J. R. Hinrichs, "A New Tool for Supervisory Self-Development," *Personnel*, July-August, 1959, pp. 46–53.

10. Beach, *Personnel: Management of People at Work*, pp. 327–28.

11. Douglas McGregor, "An Uneasy Look at Performance Appraisal" *Harvard Business Review*, May-June, 1957, p. 90.

12. Lee Stockford and H. W. Bissell, "Factors Involved in Establishing a Merit-Rating Scale," *Personnel*, September, 1949, p. 97.

13. The steps presented represent the ideas of several advocates of the joint target-setting/appraisal by results process. See especially McGregor, *The Human Side of Enterprise*, pp. 61–76.

10

Supervising the Disadvantaged: The Challenge of Human Potential

We decided to include this chapter because of the increased emphasis in business on recruiting, hiring, and training the disadvantaged worker—that is, the worker who has been either underemployed, based on his abilities, or who has lived and worked in an environment that stultifies human growth and development. This emphasis received its first impetus during the decade of 1960s, partly as a result of the civil rights movement with its national focus on extreme poverty of many of our citizens and their lack of equal opportunities. Both the nation and business became aware that in a period of affluence there were still areas of poverty so great that "they could not be attributed to temporary oscillation in the economy or to shiftlessness of the poor but only to defects in the economy and social structure itself."[1] Thus, the 1964 Civil Rights Act made it "unlawful for an employer to fail or refuse to hire, or for him to discharge or otherwise discriminate against any individual with respect to his compensation, terms, conditions, or privileges of employment because of race, color, religion, sex, or national origin."[2] And the 1962 Manpower Development and Training Act established a nationwide program of occupational training for unemployed and underemployed workers.

American business corporations have supported the federal poverty programs and pledged to hire and train the hard-core unemployed. Indeed, a recent survery of executives in the 750 largest American Corporations found that 83 percent thought private industry should be doing more in recruiting and training the unskilled and unemployables.[3]

HIRING AND TRAINING THE DISADVANTAGED: A HYPOTHETICAL CASE

Let us present a hypothetical case of a large corporation that made the decision to hire and train the disadvantaged, and explore the problems it encountered. Perhaps we can show why many corporations have been unsuccessful in this area, so that we can avoid these pitfalls and develop a successful program.[4]

The XYZ Corporation is a medium-sized company with plants throughout the United States; its home office is in New York City. The corporation has embarked on a successful program to acquire smaller firms to supplement and complement its primary product line. Although the corporation has prided itself on being an equal-opportunity employer, there are few blacks in managerial positions.

One day James Morton, vice-president of personnel and industrial relations, heard a black speaker urge that it was not only good business but the social responsibility of business to use its resources to upgrade job opportunities for the underprivileged. He cited statistics from several corporations that had engaged in programs of hiring and training hard-core unemployed and stated that after training their productivity was equal to that of the rest of the labor force. This speech so impressed Vice-President Morton that the next day he met with the company president to discuss the feasibility of hiring hard-core unemployed in ten plants in large cities around the country. In making his presentation, Morton stressed five points:

—that market research showed that minorities made up an increasing market for the firm's products, and thus publicity about programs to hire hard-core unemployed would be good business, since many of these unemployed were blacks and those with Spanish surnames;

—that unofficial statistics revealed that the corporation got about seven percent of its labor force from minority groups;

—that in most of the large cities the labor market was tight, and hiring unemployed and underemployed workers would be tapping a new source of labor supply;

—that federally funded programs to recruit and train disadvantaged workers would take the initial burden of costs off the corporation.

—that in the name of corporate responsibility the corporation could help turn unemployed workers into productive workers and thus help alleviate the urban crisis and lessen the fear of racial violence.

The president was favorably impressed with the presentation, and after a discussion with top-ranking officers, it was decided to try a pilot program in the St. Louis plant. If it proved successful, the program would be extended to the other nine cities. Accordingly, Morton was instructed to work with the St. Louis plant manager and local personnel manager in initiating the program to train and hire the hard core unemployed.

The Pilot Program

Acquired in 1963, the St. Louis plant manufactured wood and metal cabinets, its largest product line being cabinets for TV sets. It employed 1,500 workers, and most of the operative employees were semiskilled. Work in producing the cabinets was partly machine paced and partly dependent on the skill of the operative employees. The plant employed approximately 20 percent minority workers, the highest percentage in the corporation. The plant had avoided unions by paying wages above the average of the industry, although the carpenter's union was trying to organize the plant.

The plant manager had been with the plant since 1958 and been manager since 1964. The personnel manager, hired in 1967, had no previous experience in personnel work, although he had been a successful high school football coach. The home office of the corporation tended to treat the St. Louis plant as a semiautonomous division. Therefore, the primary control had been to focus on the end results of profits, sales, and return on investment. Since these end results had been satisfactory, there had been little interference in the local plant's operations. As Vice-President of Personnel, Morton had only a functional relationship with the plant manager and the personnel manager; that is to say the personnel manager's boss was the plant manager, not James Morton.

Vice-President Morton went to St. Louis to discuss the pilot project, and after some initial resistance, the plant and personnel managers agreed to initiate it. They decided to use a local community action program (CAP) agency that had had considerable experience in manpower programs in St. Louis ghetto areas. Using federal funds, the CAP agency would recruit and screen disadvantaged St. Louis blacks. The plant's minimum education requirement was the equivalent of the seventh grade in reading and writing. If recruits failed to meet this test, they attended adult education classes until they met the criterion, and then they were channeled back into the program. If they initially met the criterion, then they received pre-employment instruction from the CAP agency. Many recruits were recent arrivals from the deep South with rural backgrounds, others with long histories as welfare recipients or being unemployed. Thus, the pre-employment instruction presumably prepared the disadvantaged for the disciplined and different world of factory work. After four weeks of pre-employment instruction, they underwent six weeks of vocational training at a local community college in the type of work they would face in the factory. Next they were given on-the-job instruction at the St. Louis plant, and after a probationary period of three weeks were placed in operative positions.

Six months after the start of the program, the plant manager wrote Morton and the president and asked that it be discontinued. Costs, he said, had increased significantly, primarily because of a high turnover rate among the disadvantaged. Also, he said, the attitude of the disadvantaged prevented them from developing into responsible workers. The president decided to send Morton to investigate.

The Investigation: What Went Wrong?

What troubled Morton was that he had been so busy in the home office that he had not followed the project as closely as he felt he should have, that he had neglected to provide guidance or direction. On arriving in St. Louis he decided to interview not only the plant and personnel managers, but others as well. The first was with the plant manager.

The Plant Manager's Story

The real problem, according to the plant manager, was that turn-over among the black disadvantaged workers was too high—40 percent quit within a month after being employed. As he saw it, "these people lack the necessary mental discipline for factory work." Despite their pre-employment instruction and the vocational training, he insisted, most of them came to the plant ill-prepared for job responsibility. Even those who stayed on had high absenteeism, and the quality of their work was not very good, "especially on Monday." Though they are supposed to have a seventh-grade reading and writing ability, he complained, some of them could hardly read and write.

"These people seem to have the attitude that the world owes them a living and it is their right to have a job in our plant," The manager said. "I don't want you to think I am prejudiced against blacks because I am not—I have a black physician friend who lives in my neighborhood. But I want to recommend that we discontinue this program. We will still hire blacks, but we will do our own screening and recruiting and take only the cream of the crop. I think you can appreciate that, from a cost standpoint, we cannot continue this program."

Let us put the rest of this discussion between Morton and the plant manager in dialogue form. Note the kind of questions Morton asks.

MORTON: What steps has the plant taken to try to solve this turnover and absenteeism problem?

PLANT MANAGER: Well, one thing we tried to avoid was to treat these people differently from our regular work force. As a result, we made the decision that these workers were going to have to hack it like anyone else—without any preferential treatment.

MORTON: How were these workers introduced to the factory when they were first hired? Were they given any orientation program?

PLANT MANAGER: Same orientation program as anyone else. Someone from the personnel department took them on a short tour of the plant, explained our policies, and then turned them over to departments where they would work.

In the department they received on-the-job training.

MORTON: Have you consulted with anyone at the CAP agency to see if they had any insights?

PLANT MANAGER: Since you brought them up, let me level with you. We think they are part of the problem. They did a poor job in screening and recruiting. The people they recruited are complete misfits. There's also a rumor CAP was supporting the carpenter's union that was trying to organize around here. Fortunately, we defeated the union, but it was close, and I know they'll try again. So, to answer your question specifically, we haven't contacted them because we don't trust them.

MORTON: Have you evaluated whether turnover among disadvantaged workers is higher under some supervisors than others? That is, have you assessed whether there might be conflicts between some supervisors and disadvantaged workers?

PLANT MANAGER: No, we haven't. Actually, under our setup, that assessment is hard to determine. We run three shifts, and to keep the supervisors' morale high, we rotate them every three weeks so no one supervisor will continually have to work the night shift.

MORTON: So workers will have a number of different supervisors over, say, six months?

PLANT MANAGER: Well, yes, the supervisors prefer it that way. And I figure the happier our supervisors are the more productive the plant will be.

MORTON: What's the turnover among the regular work force?

PLANT MANAGER: About 20 percent a year, which frankly is a little high for our industry. But I want to stress that we have high production and are making the corporation a good return on investment.

MORTON: Have you conducted exit interviews with the disadvantaged workers who quit to find out their reasons for leaving?

PLANT MANAGER: I think we have, but you'll have to talk with the personnel manager.

The Personnel Manager's Story

MORTON: What do you think are the reasons there is such
high turnover among the disadvantaged workers?

PERSONNEL MANAGER: Well, our records show that 60
percent of these people have been in St. Louis less than a
year and have farm backgrounds. They come from Tennessee,
Arkansas, and Mississippi. They are just not used to factory
work and are looking for payday and sundown. Moreover,
they've been indoctrinated with a militant attitude that whites
can't be trusted and they resent any form of discipline. So
when our supervisors crack down on them, they quit, simple
as that.

MORTON: Do you have a grievance procedure so a worker
may appeal a disciplinary action if he thinks it's unfair?

PERSONNEL MANAGER: Yes, it's in our policy manual. If
the worker feels unfairly treated by his supervisor, he can go
to the next high level of management, the production superintendent. If he is not satisfied at this step, he can appeal
directly to me.

MORTON: Has any disadvantaged worker ever used the
grievance procedure?

PERSONNEL MANAGER: There has been only one case
appealed to my level. A black disadvantaged worker complained that his foreman, Sam Jones, cursed him on the job.
Sam said "Hey, you black S.O.B., quit goofing off and start
working!" Sam is a little hard-nosed in his supervision, but
he gets the work out. He also tends to cuss out anybody, black
or white, who is not working. But I counseled Sam and told
him to tone it down, and we've had no more complaints.

MORTON: Do you conduct exit interviews with workers
who quit to determine their reasons?

PERSONNEL MANAGER: Well, quite frankly, in regard to
the disadvantaged workers, not very many. When they quit,
they just don't show up for work. They call in to the payroll
department to give them an address to send a check to. Also,
the union organizing campaign kept me and my staff busy.

MORTON: Have you talked with the CAP agency about
the problem?

PERSONNEL MANAGER: One of their manpower specialists called on me to discuss the problem and tried to lay the
blame on our supervisors as being racists. I don't buy that
viewpoint. I think the failure rests with the manpower com-
ponent in their recruiting and training program.

MORTON: Do you have any black supervisors?

PERSONNEL MANAGER: Yes, we recently appointed one,
and he is going to work out for us. He has been with us a long
time and is not a trouble maker.

MORTON: Have you initiated any supervisory training
programs concerned with leadership, motivation, and human
relations?

PERSONNEL MANAGER: Well, a year ago we showed the
supervisors a series of films on these subjects, but that's about
it.

MORTON: Perhaps I could talk to the supervisor you
mentioned, Sam Jones.

Supervisor Jones's Story

MORTON: I'm told you really get the work out of your
men. What do you consider the main factor in your success?

JONES: I believe in doing an honest day's work for an
honest day's pay. I worked hard as a kid on my folks' farm in
the Ozarks and I know what hard work is. I didn't get a whole
lot of education, and I appreciate the opportunity this company has given me. I aim to make the best of it. Any man
under me better work and give this company a fair day's work
for a fair day's pay, or I'll be on them like white on rice.

MORTON: Maybe you can give me an honest answer.
What do you think of these disadvantaged workers the company hired?

JONES: Not much. Niggers are different and just won't
work. You can't get them to do anything. Give them half a
chance and they'll goof off.

MORTON: Do you feel this way about all Negroes?

JONES: Not all, just these here young smart-alecky ones.
Why just the other day one of them passed another one in
the plant and gave him a clenched-fist salute. Everyone knows

that means they want to overthrow the government. Now, if the production superintendent had backed me, I would have fired him on the spot.

MORTON: Do you recall who gave the clenched-fist salute and if he is still working in the plant?

JONES: Yes, sir, his name is Henry Odum and as far as I know, he's still in the plant.

Worker Odum's Story

Morton made arrangements through the personnel manager to talk with Odum. Initially, he did not want to speak out, but after being assured his job was not in jeopardy, he consented.

MORTON: Why do you think there is such a high turnover among the workers that come through the CAP agency's recruitment and training program?

ODUM: Well, when I come up here six months ago from Mississippi and couldn't find a job, I signed up with CAP and they gave us special training. All during our training we were treated decently; I learned to take pride in being black. But once we started working, things went wrong—name calling, cussing, "nigger," "black S.O.B.," it all comes out. I know cases where a worker called "boy" is several years older than his supervisor. That's the reason why black workers don't stay here. Sometimes I think I had it better back in Mississippi.

MORTON: What does it mean when you give another black a clenched-fist salute?

ODUM: That's a greeting saying I'm proud to be black.

MORTON: In your opinion, are all the white supervisors prejudiced against blacks?

ODUM: Not all. In fact, right now I've got a good white supervisor, Mr. Globetti, who treats everybody equally, but next week he's going to be rotated to another shift.

MORTON: Are most of the CAP-trained employees interested in and capable of doing the work in this factory?

ODUM: Yes, sir, most, but not all. A few may not want to work, but the great majority of us do. As for as capable, yes sir, the vocational training was a lot more difficult than the work in this factory.

Supervisor Globetti's Story

After checking with the personnel manager and Gerald Globetti's production superintendent, Morton then talked with Globetti.

MORTON: I understand that you are one of the outstanding supervisors in your division. What do you attribute your success to?

GLOBETTI: Well, sir, that's good to hear. I've never been told that before. As far as any success as a supervisor, I try to support the men I'm working with. I try to treat them fair and square and call on my more experienced workers to help train and develop the less experienced workers.

MORTON: How have you found the CAP trainees as workers?

GLOBETTI: Not bad. In fact, most of them are well trained. Some of them are reluctant to speak out or ask questions about anything they don't understand about the work or the equipment. So I try to make it a point to stress we don't expect them to know everything at once and check with them from time to time to see how things are going.

MORTON: What do you think causes the high turnover among the workers from the CAP program?

GLOBETTI: Quite frankly, I think there are two reasons. One, the shifting about of supervisors; you can't really get to know your men and vice-versa if you shift around so much. Two, some of our supervisors are just biased against black workers.

MORTON: What percentage would you estimate are biased?

GLOBETTI: Roughly 40 percent. Some of them are not complete racists, but they've been influenced by the attitudes of the other supervisors.

MORTON: Were the supervisors given any special training in working with the trainees?

GLOBETTI: None at all.

Morton conferred again with the plant manager and personnel manager, indicating he wanted to study the interview results before making a final decision on whether to continue or discontinue the program. He also talked to the manpower personnel of the CAP program, and concluded that the primary blame for the high turnover rested with the St. Louis plant and not with CAP.

We will leave it to the reader to determine what recommendations Vice-President Morton probably would have decided on, for sometimes it is easier to diagnose the problem than to implement a plan to solve it—especially when the problem is compounded by the attitudes and prejudices of many people involved.

OVERCOMING BARRIERS TO EMPLOYING THE DISADVANTAGED

Every situation is different, of course, and this applies to different organizations attempting to plan and implement programs of hiring disadvantaged workers. Nevertheless, there are some general concepts and insights that have been gained through research and experience in this area.

Disadvantaged workers come primarily from minority groups that have been discriminated against, such as blacks, Indians, Mexican-Americans, Puerto Ricans, and Appalachian whites. We will focus primarily on blacks because they form the largest single group and because most of the research has focused on black disadvantaged workers.

As we have seen in Vice-President Morton's case, one major barrier is the difference in attitudes between top management and successively lower levels of management regarding whether it is desirable to hire disadvantaged workers. Table 1 shows the

Table 1. Management Support for Special Hiring

Question: Do you think companies should make a special effort to hire and train Negroes for skilled jobs, or isn't this a company responsibility?

MANAGEMENT LEVEL	YES, COMPANIES HAVE RESPONSIBILITY	NO, NOT A COMPANY RESPONSIBILITY
Fourth & fifth (top)	100%	0
Third	84%	12%
Second	65%	33%
First (lowest level)	51%	44%

Note: "No Opinion" category omitted.

Source: 1968 confidential study conducted among 314 managers in a leading company. See Joseph R. Goeke and Caroline S. Weymar, "Barriers to Hiring the Blacks," *Harvard Business Review,* September-October, 1969, p. 146.

attitudes of the managers in one company on this subject. The skill of the first-line supervisor in working with and through people is a major factor in any such program. This skill is important, of course, in supervising any employee, but it is especially acute in supervising the black worker. Here's how one black management consultant points out the dilemma:

> Too often the white supervisor is the only management link with the black employee. Not only is the white supervisor improperly trained to deal on a human basis with those responsible to him, but he frequently comes to his job with a fixed set of prejudices against all blacks. He may not like the black employee's mode of dress or his Afro haircut and, as a white, he can have difficulty understanding his own fears and insecurities when dealing with the black employee. Today's young black is less likely to hide his frustration and hostility from the white man. This can create an environment in which neither the supervisor nor the employee makes a serious attempt to reach a level of cooperation that can lead to better performance.[5]

Still another major barrier to hiring blacks is that they score lower than whites on many employment tests, although research indicates that despite lower scores they perform on the job just as well as whites.[6] This finding would tend to support lowering employment standards for disadvantaged blacks, yet as Table 2

Table 2. Management Support for Lowering Employment Qualifications.

Question: How do you feel about lowering the company's employment qualifications in order to hire more people from disadvantaged groups? Do you think it is proper or not proper?

MANAGEMENT LEVEL	YES, PROPER TO LOWER EMPLOYMENT QUALIFICATIONS	NO, NOT PROPER TO LOWER THEM
Fourth & Fifth (top)	78%	22%
Third	40%	60%
Second	23%	76%
First (lowest level)	16%	84%

Note: "No opinion" category omitted.

Source: 1968 confidential study conducted among 314 managers in a leading company. See Joseph R. Goeke and Caroline S. Weymar, "Barriers to Hiring the Blacks," *Harvard Business Review*, September-October, 1969, p. 149.

shows, here again there is extreme resentment by lower-level managers and other rank-and-file employees.

Finally, a major barrier is the background and attitudes of the disadvantaged workers themselves. Let's face it—they have been isolated from the mainstream of American life; they are suspicious of business motives, or of almost any white's motives, for that matter. They are often preoccupied with personal problems. Many are poorly educated and lack skills. As a result, they have not experienced many successes in the accepted meaning of the term and their heroes, as one observer put it, tend to be "the brother who messes with the system and gets away with it."[7]

There are two basic concerns in making a program of hiring the disadvantaged work: help them prepare and adjust to the world of work and help the company prepare and adjust to them. The behavior of the supervisors is especially critical in helping the company's adjustment, and we hope the concepts presented in this book will help you in managing disadvantaged workers. Let us now see how pertinent the "hierarchy of needs" concept is to the disadvantaged worker.

The Disadvantaged Worker and the Hierarchy of Needs

The hard-core disadvantaged workers are extremely suspicious, but once this suspicion is overcome, Maslow's "hierarchy of needs" concept seems to apply. One study states that, "it would appear that the hard core have motivations and goals similar to workers in general; where they differ, it seems to be due to the failures that the hard core have experienced rather than to different subcultural values."[8]

One company that directly confronts the problem of past failures is Con-Edison Corporation, the big Eastern utility, which stresses the need of involvement on the part of the trainees. At the outset trainees tour facilities to see the jobs that await them. Also in the first week of orientation there are sessions dealing with success and failure. Here's how the chairman of Con-Edison has described these sessions:

> First we ask trainees for examples of where they think they have failed in their lives. We do not dwell on this, but we do ask them what they have learned from their failures—perhaps

something they can share with the rest of the group to help them avoid the same trouble.

We do, however, bore in on the success stories. We want to know how the trainee felt at a particular moment of success, how long it lasted, and the like.

We emphasize success for a very simple reason; most of our ghetto youths are more familiar with failure. We want them to think how it feels to be successful. For many of them, this program can be their first big success. We tell them that too.[9]

A training director who has had success in getting supervisors to use motivation theory in working with the disadvantaged is Alan Hamline of Thiokol Chemical Corporation. He has found that disadvantaged workers are not as likely to be initially motivated on the job by higher level needs or self-fulfillment, esteem, or even social needs. His experience has shown that the newly hired hard-core worker is most concerned about safety needs (security, avoidance of threats and anxieties) and physiological needs (food, sleep). Thus, a supervisor who greets his newly hired disadvan-taged workers with a pep talk emphasizing the importance of "doing your best for the company team" is missing the boat. The supervisor is appealing to a higher level need, when the worker will be most concerned with things like: "Can I trust this supervisor?" "Should I believe what he says?" "Will I get a fair shake from him?" "If I make a mistake will I get fired?" Only after the lower level concerns of the worker are satisfied will he be motivated by appeals to team-work, helping others, and higher esteem and fulfillment needs.[10]

Creating a Positive Company Environment

Motivation theory is useful not only in helping the disadvantaged in their transition to the world of work, but also in creating within the company a positive environment for them. For example, any company initiating such a program should first communicate to all employees the nature of the program, its goals, and how it will be implemented. Not only should this information be com-municated, but the employees affected—especially first-line supervisors—should have an opportunity to contribute their opinons about the program.

One of the best ways is to have a session with the supervisors prior to the program to describe it in detail and explore the role of the supervisor in it. The supervisors should be allowed to discuss anticipated problems and raise questions—such as these, which came out of one session: "Can we use normal disciplinary measures with these workers?" "How do I answer my men if they express the view that the hard-core are getting preferential treatment?" "How do I deal with prejudice among my men?"[11] In addition, it helps to have follow-up sessions after the start of the program.

Successful Training of the Disadvantaged

As we stressed earlier, not only must the company environment be prepared for the trainees but the trainees must be prepared for the company. Lockheed Aircraft Corporation had successful programs in its plants in Marietta, Georgia, and Sunnyvale, California, two of the largest plants in the corporation. Here are some of the reasons instructors and observers gave for the training success:

1. The training developed proficiency for specific jobs, jobs for which the trainees knew they were being prepared.
2. The students were prepared for skill levels slightly above those required by the jobs for which they were being trained.
3. The job instruction was by demonstration. Most poor and uneducated people have few associative hooks on which to hang new information. They do not learn well by association. They must be taught by showing, by doing, and by repetition.
4. Recognition was frequent. The training was set up in small units of work.
5. The trainees were given special personal help. Stanley Hawkins, an LMSC training supervisor, estimates that he spent up to 50 percent of his time on personal problems, ranging from bailing trainees out of jail in the middle of the night to working with creditors to get garnishments reduced.
6. There were jobs in sight. It is important to have a job ready for successful trainees.
7. The jobs were not dead-end jobs.[12]

Points one and seven are crucial: unless there are jobs at the end of the training and unless there are opportunities for advancement, a company should not engage in such a program.

GIVING DISADVANTAGED WORKERS PREFERENTIAL TREATMENT

Should disadvantaged workers be given preferential treatment? Table 2 indicated that 78 percent of top management in one company felt that employment standard should be lowered for disadvantaged workers, whereas 84 percent of first-level managers felt it should not be lowered. Assuming that the employment qualifications are realistic for the company's jobs, on this issue we will have to side with the first-level managers. The first-line supervisors are the ones who will be directly working with the disadvantaged, not top management. If the supervisors are not committed to the program, they can sabotage it no matter how committed top management is. Moreover, the supervisors are held accountable for meeting production standards and quotas. Thus, is it really fair to them to hire unqualified employees?

On the other hand, we feel that companies should make a special effort to recruit, train, and develop disadvantaged workers so that they will not remain disadvantaged. Thus, we endorse remedial training and education programs to help the disadvantaged measure up to the company's employment standards. To a certain extent this represents preferential treatment, and in fact in one company, the backlash from rank and file workers to a program of hiring the disadvantaged resulted because they did not have the opportunity for these special programs. But this backlash of presumed preferential treatment could easily be eliminated. As the chief executive officer of one company concludes: "Considering the evidence of success already shown in the hard-core program, perhaps we should start giving all new employees the same kind of orientation, motivation and training."[13]

SUMMARY

This chapter highlighted positive steps some business firms may take to make job opportunities more equal for the disadvantaged. A case study focusing on the problems facing disadvantaged workers was presented. Finally, after discussion of additional barriers, which show the problem is not an easy one, we presented some ways of overcoming them.

One major barrier is the discrepancy in attitudes between top and lower management as to whether it is desirabale to hire disadvantaged workers. Lack of training of first-line supervisors in human-resource management also causes difficulties. Another barrier is that even though research indicates that blacks do well on the job, many times they score lower on employment tests than do whites. Finally, because of their past, many disadvantaged workers have attitudes that cause them to be distrustful of whites.

A successful way to overcome the barriers is to introduce programs that help the disadvantaged adjust to the world of work and the company adjust to them. Especially important is building on successes and utilizing learning by doing in the training process. In creating a positive environment it is important to involve lower levels of management early in the program and give them an opportunity to discuss anticipated problems and raise questions. Finally, it is important that courses in human-resource management be required of all supervisors.

QUESTIONS

1. Assume you are Vice-President Morton. Based on the facts derived from your interviews, develop a recommended plan of action to remedy the situation in the St. Louis plant. Support your reasoning.
2. In Table 1, 57 percent of top management thought companies should make a special effort to hire and train Negroes for skilled jobs, but 100 percent of the lowest level supervisors thought not. What do you think explains the discrepancy in top management's thinking and lower level management? Which position do you support and why?
3. Utilizing but not limited to motivation theory, explain the causes and discuss possible solutions for the high unemployment among the disadvantaged.
4. Assume that top management makes a decision to hire a number of disadvantaged workers (25 percent of the work force) for a private manufacturing concern. Further assume that after the introduction of the disadvantaged workers, economic costs increase. Speculate as to the reasons why top management made the decisions to recruit and hire disadvantaged workers. Speculate as to the reasons why the economic costs have increased. Based on this speculation, what should top management do to deal with this situation?

NOTES

1. *Training and Jobs for the Urban Poor* (New York: Committee for Economic Development, 1970), p. 9.

2. Title VII, Equal Opportunity Civil Rights Act of 1964.

3. Joseph R. Goeke and Caroline S. Weymar, "Barriers to Hiring the Blacks," *Harvard Business Review*, September-October, 1969, pp. 144–152.

4. The idea for this hypothetical case comes from a report prepared for Mississippi Employment Security Commission by Charles W. Roe, "Supervising the Disadvantaged," Department of Management, Mississippi State University, April, 1970 (unpublished study).

5. W. Victor Rouse, "The Frustrated Black Worker," *Business Horizons*, April, 1971, p. 27.

6. Richard S. Barrett, "Gray Areas in Black and White Testing," *Harvard Business Review*, January-February, 1968, pp. 92–95.

7. Joseph White, "Toward a Black Psychology," *Ebony*, September 1970, p. 49.

8. R. A. Hudson Rosen, "The World of Work Through the Eyes of the Hard Core," *Personnel Administration*, May-June, 1970, pp. 8–21.

9. Charles F. Luce, "We Hire the Hard-Core Unemployed," *Dun's Review*, February, 1969, pp. 51–52.

10. Alan L. Hamline, "Will Maslow Work with the Hard-Core?", *Training in Business and Industry*, March, 1969, pp. 71–72.

11. Newton Marqulies, "An Integrated Approach to Supervisory Training for Hiring the Hard-Core," *Training and Development Journal*, August, 1970, p. 43.

12. James D. Hodgson and Marshall H. Brenner, "Successful Experience: Training Hard-Core Unemployed," *Harvard Business Review*, September-October, 1968, pp. 152–153.

13. Luce, "We Hire the Hard-Core Unemployed," p. 52.

11

Incompetent Management Versus Enlightened Management: How to Beat the Peter Principle

The Peter Principle, a 1969 best seller by Lawrence Peter and Raymond Hull,[1] is a satirical yet also serious analysis of incompetence in organizations, an in-depth look at what the authors call *hierarchiology*—the study of hierarchies. In analyzing hundreds of cases of occupational incompetence, they state, they have seen the same phenomenon occurring over and over: a competent person in a lower position in a hierarchy is promoted to a higher position and becomes incompetent. The competent student becomes incompetent as a teacher. The competent teacher becomes incompetent as a department head. The competent department head becomes incompetent once he is promoted. And so on.

From this analysis they formulated *The Peter Principle*, which states "In a hierarchy every employee tends to rise to his level of incompetence." A corollary is "in time, every post tends to be occupied by an employee who is incompetent to carry out its duties."

THE PETER PRINCIPLE: EVIDENCE PRO AND CON

The best evidence to support this principle comes from our own experience. All of us can point to numerous cases where the principle seems to be operating. One group vice-president in an organization whose specialty is buying other companies has stated, "I sincerely feel that at least half of the companies in the U.S. are poorly managed."[2] that is, that there are a large number of incompetent managers in industry. Perhaps this is what Henri Fayol was guarding against when he stated that one of the principles of command is "to eliminate the incompetent."[3] Thus, the Peter Principle seems to be operating on a rather broad scale. Certainly when executives or students discuss the principle, they invariably seem to agree with it. They see it as an explanation as to why so many institutions are less than effective and why so many people in organizations show tendencies of incompetent behavior.

Some behavioral scientists disagree with this view, saying that the problem with most institutions and organizations is not that people are reaching their levels of incompetence, but that organizations are full of people at all levels who have contributions to make to occupational and organizational goals but who are being stifled because of the nature of the institutions. The specific criticism is that our institutions and organizations are making use of outmoded organizational theories, management philosophies, and leadership styles, which may have been appropriate at one time but that no longer are in today's world of rapid social and technological change. To illustrate, when Robert Townsend became President of Avis Rent A Car, he was assured that no one on his top management team was any good and that his first job should be to recruit new management. The advice seemed sound since Avis had not made a profit in thirteen years. But, wrote Townsend, "three years later the company had grown internally from $30 million sales to $75 million sales, and had made successive annual profits of $1 million, $3 million, and $5 million"[4]—and the amazing thing is that this success was accomplished with the same team that had been labeled incompetent. In his book *Up the Organization,* Townsend attributes the success to removing the undesirable aspects of bureaucracy and the use of a participative management philosophy.

Management writer Larry Greiner has indicated that one way

to bring successful change in a stagnating organization is to bring in a new man, known for his ability to introduce improvements, as the official head of the organization.[5] However, as social psychologist Rensis Likert has demonstrated, in most cases it takes years before the deterioration of human resources caused by an obsolete management system is reflected in the end results of profits, sales, productivity, and so on.

The question is, what can a manager or supervisor do when he suspects that the Peter Principle may be operating in his organization or department? What can he do when he suspects that as head of the unit he may be losing his grip on things, even reaching *his* level of incompetence? The answer depends on whether he is a chief executive or a middle or lower level manager. If he is a chief executive, the answer is probably *organizational development*, a concept we will explore in the next chapter. If he is a middle or lower level manager, the answer is enlightened management.

ENLIGHTENED MANAGEMENT: A SYNTHESIS OF VIEWPOINTS

The successful practice of enlightened management will in many situations make the Peter Principle invalid. Enlightened management is having the ability to draw from the body of management knowledge so that you can carry out the management process of planning, organizing, supervising, and controlling. More precisely, it ensures that you do not become obsolete in a supervisory position and that you continue to be effective in working with and through people.

Thus, enlightened management tries to create an environment, formulate a philosophy, and utilize a leadership style that focuses on individual and group performance and individual and group development, so that they will complement and support the organization's objectives. The entire thrust of this book has been to help you successfully practice enlightened management in appropriate situations, to release the human energy, stimulate development, and utilize teamwork to move toward the organization's goals.

Figure 21 shows a synthesis of enlightened management concepts; it portrays the relationships between Maslow's need hierarchy, Herzberg's motivation-hygiene theory, leadership

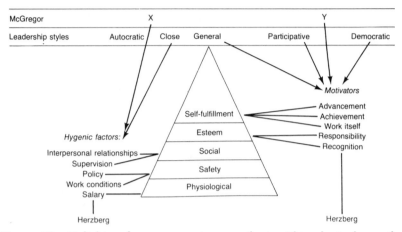

Figure 21. Enlightened management—a synthesis. This chart shows the relationship between Maslow's need hierarchy, Herzberg's hygiene-motivation theory, leadership styles, and McGregor's X and Y philosophies.

styles, and McGregor's X and Y theory.[7] A basic premise of enlightened management is that in developed countries most people have their lower level needs relatively well satisfied, and so managers often fall down on the job by not motivating people through providing opportunities for higher level need satisfaction—needs that are insatiable. Another premise, one that is contrary to the Peter Principle, is that people at all levels have contributions to make and untapped potential that has not been realized. Figure 21, then, represents the theory and concepts advocated by many behavioral scientists as a frame of reference for working with and through people. The figure shows that a type of participative management system and leadership style is desirable in working with and through people—in effect, a system or style where there is power sharing between supervisors and subordinates.

The Case Against Enlightened Management

There are, however, different viewpoints and certain qualifications in attempting to utilize enlightened management. One articulate critic of enlightened management is management theorist George Strauss, who believes (1) that it unduly emphasizes the universality of the self-fulfillment need level; (2) that the job, rather than the home or the community may not be the primary area of need satisfaction; and (3) that too little attention has been given to evaluating the potential gains of enlightened management as opposed to the costs of introducing it into an organization that has not been practicing it.

Another criticism is that it would be difficult to apply enlightened management in parts of the world where most of the population have limited educations and where they are still struggling to satisfy basic needs. Moreover, an insecure or unskilled manager attempting to apply enlightened management may slide over into permissive management and then, in trying to regain control, revert to an autocratic approach. Finally, it is said, not all situations lend themselves to enlightened management. For example, in highly routinized work that is subject to possible automation, it would not be economically feasible to use this approach. Also, as we showed in the chapter on supervision, there are certain situations that dictate either autocratic or close supervision, especially in the short run.

The Case for Enlightened Management

Despite the above criticisms, we still believe that enlightened management can make the Peter Principle inoperative and is the management style to strive for in developed countries in most situations. We reach this conclusion for four reasons.

First, in developed countries and especially in the United States the population is becoming better and better educated. The greater the education people have, the more they expect to have involvement and challenge in their work and jobs.

Second, with the accelerating rate of new knowledge and change in our society it naturally follows that a person will need to be able to adjust and adapt and innovate. This adaptability can best be accomplished through a shared approach and through working in an environment that encourages teamwork, rewards achievement and innovation, and encourages openness in communication.

Third, even in organizations where half the people (because of past experience or an unusually strong security need) actually prefer a more closely supervised approach, we feel enlightened management is still better because it will give achievement-oriented employees a chance to grow and assume responsibility and make less achievement-oriented people become more achievement oriented.

Finally, a manager must do more than just supervise his own department. He must spend time planning, coordinating with other departments, selling ideas to higher levels, writing reports, attending meetings, dealing with problem areas and exploring alternatives, and doing a certain amount of public relations work. Unless he is an enlightened manager who delegates and depends on his staff, how will he find time to spend on these other activities? How can he be sure that the regular work is being done properly when he is absent from his department?

ENLIGHTENED AND UNENLIGHTENED MANAGEMENT IN PRACTICE: THE CAREERS OF TWO MANAGERS

To show enlightened and unenlightened management in practice, let us follow the careers of two managers in a hypothetical company, a nationwide insurance firm headquartered in New York City. Several years earlier a top executive heard a psychologist state that there appeared to be a direct relationship between a person's need and desire for achievement and his success as a manager and that it was possible to measure this need and desire for achievement. The executive thereupon hired the psychologist to design a test to measure a person's need for achievement. The test was given to incoming college graduates entering a managerial training program, and after five years the test results were compared with how well the college graduates had performed as managers. The results indicated that a person with a high need for achievement was indeed more likely to be successful as a manager than a person who scored low on the need for achievement. However, a disturbing aspect was that 40 percent who scored high on need for achievement proved unsuccessful as managers. The psychologist advised the executive, therefore, that because of this finding the achievement test be used as only one factor in initial screening for managerial trainees. He strongly advised against using the test as a basis for making decisions regarding promotions to management positions.

With this background in mind, let us now examine the careers of two managerial trainees during this five-year period.

Jackson's Career: Unenlightened Management

James Jackson scored the highest on the achievement test of any managerial trainee. The son of a sales manager for a pharmaceutical company, Jackson had since high school been oriented toward a career in sales. His father, convinced that competition is what makes capitalism a successful economic system and that competition brings out the best in people, encouraged Jackson to compete in athletics and in academic pursuits. Since in team sports Jackson was initially unsuccessful, he concentrated his efforts in sports based on individual skill such as golf and tennis. In these areas he was highly successful, and in school work he always ranked in the top 10 percent of his class. In college he chose marketing as his major.

Upon graduation Jackson went to work for the insurance company, and after completing the managerial training program became an insurance salesman and a highly successful one. Eighteen months later, higher management concluded that he was a comer and promoted him to district sales manager, in a territory where past sales had been assessed as mediocre and far below potential. Jackson called in his twelve salesmen, gave them a pep talk on the virtues of competition, and initiated a competitive program by which the top three salesmen would receive prizes each month and the bottom three would receive a tail-ender plaque; the rankings of all salesmen were posted each month on the office bulletin board.

Higher management was quite pleased to note that in the first three months of Jackson's tenure, sales increased appreciably. This initial success motivated James to greater efforts to increase performance by having meetings twice a month, during which he would give pep talks, drawing from inspirational, "how to get rich quick" books, and strongly urged his men to enroll in a course on "how to motivate and influence people."

After six months of increase, sales began leveling off and even declining. At this point Jackson started sending tags to salesmen's homes requesting that the wife place tags on the furniture reminding husbands of the new furniture they could win in the new promotion campaign. But much to his dismay, sales continued to decline, and the more he tried to stop the reversal the more turnover among salesmen increased. Finally, the point was reached where sales were below the average under the previous sales manager. At this point, higher management offered James a choice: either accept a demotion to salesman or leave the company.

Tyler's Career: Enlightened Management

John Tyler scored the second highest of any managerial trainee on the achievement test. His father died when Tyler was seven and so his mother was the greatest single influence in his life. Fortunately, she did not tie him to her apron strings but encouraged him to grow and to pursue various interests. She actively encouraged him to read and to examine conflicting points of view. As a result, Tyler became an open-minded person unusually free of prejudice toward people and ideas. He was also an excellent student, and in college majored in speech and became a member of the debating team. He was keenly interested in sports and although not an active participant on a varsity team, served as manager of the basketball team his junior and senior years.

Two college experiences later influenced his career with the insurance company. First, he took a course on "small-group dynamics," which was concerned with small-group problem solving and the inner workings of group behavior, and this convinced Tyler that under certain conditions a group could produce a better solution to a problem than could an individual. Second, the school's losing basketball team hired a new coach who used an entirely different approach from his predecessor and constantly stressed the importance of teamwork rather than that everyone try to be a scoring leader. The squad met frequently and discussed how they could improve teamwork and individual performances, and in effect members of the team shared the leadership and coaching with their coach. The result was a more successful season.

When Tyler joined the insurance company after graduation, his early career was much like Jackson's. After two years in the field as a salesman, he was appointed sales manager of a district rated below average in sales. In his first month, he made it a point to get to know individually all his salesmen. He tried to develop a supportive relationship with the salesmen so that they would look on him as a source of assistance. He had concluded that, like his basketball team, a problem in the past was that the salesmen were competing with each other instead of focusing on an overall goal and competing with other companies. As a result, there had been considerable secrecy among the salesmen regarding prospects, successful sales techniques, and so on. Tyler tried to create an environment of cooperation so that the group competed against overall sales targets and other insurance companies. He did so by having regular monthly educational meetings where members learned from one another as well as from him. During these meetings he introduced team and individual target settings where everyone shared in setting the overall sales quota and listened to targets developed by individuals. They also had role-playing sessions where they conducted simulated sales calls and coached each other on how to improve. Tyler also established a group bonus system for members of the team to share (in addition to their individual commissions), and over time the team members began sharing all sorts of information and ideas and developed high morale. They began setting high sales objectives, and after a year they became the number one sales division in the corporation.

SUMMARY

In this chapter we presented the Peter Principle, which seems to contradict many of the things we have been saying. The Peter Principle, if interpreted literally, is a pessimistic view of the capabilities of man. A more optimistic view comes from behavioral scientists—that with the practice of enlightened management in appropriate situations, the Peter Principle will be inoperative.

The Peter Principle contends that in a mature organization people will be promoted until they reach their level of incompetence. Our thesis is that in a mature organization people at various levels are operating at only about 50 percent of their potential. Thus, the problem is not that people have reached their level of incompetence, rather that the proper environment has not been created that focuses on performance and development that helps people realize their potential through work. For example, the design of an organization structure and the use of leadership styles allow people satisfaction through work itself, increased responsibility, recognition, achievement, and the opportunity for self-fulfillment.

QUESTIONS

1. Support or rebut the Peter Principle, based on your own observations and experience. Include an explanation of the principle itself.
2. What is the argument of behavioral scientists in opposition to the Peter Principle?
3. What can a manager do when he suspects that the Peter Principle may be operating in his organization? Consider different management levels.
4. What is the authors' concept of enlightened management? Is it of practical use to you?
5. What type of leadership style did Jackson use in attempting to achieve effective results? Elaborate on why he failed.
6. What type of leadership style did Tyler use in attempting to achieve effective results? Elaborate on why he succeeded.
7. Do you think top management of the insurance company should share in the failure of Jackson as a manager? Why or why not?
8. When new salesmen are hired in Tyler's division, how do you think they would be trained? If after three months a new salesman was not meeting an average quota, how do you think the situation would be handled? If after six months, the same salesman was still not meeting an average sales quota, how do you think the situation would be handled?
9. Do you think Tyler's approach would work with salesmen in all companies? Defend your reasoning.

NOTES

1. Lawrence Peter and Raymond Hull, *The Peter Principle* (New York: William Morrow and Company, 1969).
2. Norman A. Berg, "What's Different About Conglomerate Management?" *Harvard Business Review*, November-December, 1969, pp. 112–20.
3. Henri Fayol, *General and Industrial Administration* (London: Sir Isaac Pitman & Sons, 1949), p. 98.
4. Robert Townsend, *Up the Organization* (New York: Alfred A. Knopf, 1970), p. 141.
5. Larry E. Griener, "Patterns of Organization Change," *Harvard Business Review*, May-June, 1967, pp. 122–23.
6. Rensis Likert, *The Human Organization* (New York: McGraw-Hill Book Company, 1967).

7. The basic idea for this figure came from the Personnel Department, IBM World Trade Corporation, Wellington, New Zealand.

8. George Strauss, "Some Notes on Power-Equalization," in Harold J. Leavitt, ed., *The Social Science of Organizations* (Englewood Cliffs, N. J.: Prentice-Hall, 1963).

Part 3

A View
From the Top

12

New Developments in Management Theory: Organization Development and the Systems Approach

Early in the book we introduced you to some traditional concepts of management theory—the unity of command principle, the span of control principle, types of authority, and the concept of delegation of authority. Some writers maintain these traditional concepts are obsolete because of newer developments in management theory. However, we have discovered in working with organizations ranging from business concerns to community action antipoverty programs that when these principles are ignored, all sorts of unnecessary problems are created. Of course, sometimes the unity of command principle, say, *must* be violated in order to best accomplish certain objectives. However, a manager should still be aware of the potential disastrous consequences because of the violation and take steps to alleviate them.

In this chapter we will introduce two newer developments in management theory—namely, organizational development and the systems approach. In presenting these newer developments we are not throwing out traditional theory but rather building on it. Anyone in a top management position must be thoroughly familiar with these concepts, but they are also of value to managers and supervisors at all levels.

ORGANIZATION DEVELOPMENT: WHAT IT IS

We stated that the practice of enlightened management by an individual manager can make the Peter Principle of incompetence invalid. However, unfortunately, sometimes an organization is so stagnated that individual managers cannot change the organization's downward trend. We can see this if we consider organizations as *systems of interdependent elements.* As other writers have indicated, "an organization is not a mechanical system in which one part can be changed without a concomitant effect on the other parts. Rather, an organizational system shares with biological systems the property of an intense interdependence of parts such that a change in one part has an impact on the others."[1] We will describe the systems approach later, but at this point let us stress that organiation development takes a systems approach in trying to improve the state of an organization.

An excellent systems model and frame of reference for understanding the concept of organizational development—which hereafter we will abbreviate "OD"—and its various strategies is shown in Figure 22. This model, developed by social psychologist Rensis Likert, groups the dimensions of a company's human organization into three broad categories or variables: *causal, intervening,* and *end-result.* He defines the three variables as follows.[2]

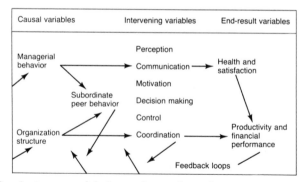

Figure 22. Systems model for understanding the concept of organization development. (Source: Rensis Likert and David G. Bowers, "Organizational Theory and Human Resources Accounting," *American Psychologist,* June, 1969, p. 587.)

Causal Variables. These independent variables "determine the course of developments within an organization and the results achieved by the organization." They include only those independent variables that can be "altered or changed by the organization and its management. General business conditions, for example, although an independent variable, is not included among the causal list. Causal variables include the structure of the organization and management's policies, decisions, business and leadership strategies, skills, and behavior."

Intervening Variables. These reflect "the internal state and health of the organization." They include, for example, "the loyalties, attitudes, motivations, performance goals, and perceptions of all members and their collective capacity for effective interaction, communication, and decision making."

End-Result Variables. These are dependent variables that reflect "the achievements of the organization, such as its productivity, costs, scrap loss, and earnings."

What Likert says is that casual variables affect intervening variables, which in turn affect end results. Thus, when an organization is running into such difficulties as declining sales and profits and high turnover and absenteeism, the problem can usually be traced to deficiencies in the causal variables of organizational structure or top management's policies, decisions, and leadership philosophies, strategies, and behavior. With Likert's framework as background, let us now examine what OD is.

OD is a relatively new concept in management theory. It is believed to have emerged around 1957 in the work of the late Douglas McGregor with Union Carbide, of a human relations research group at Esso, and of the Survey Science Research Center at the University of Michigan in its efforts to change organizations through attitude surveys and feedback of results to management for diagnosis and corrective action.[3] The better known theorist-practitioners of OD define it as a process of positively changing an organization over time so that it shifts from one state to an improved state of development. By "development" we mean, for a business firm, end-results in productivity, financial performance, and increased satisfactions of organizational members. For a non-profit organization, development would be improved realization of the organization's objectives, whatever they might be.

The objectives of typical OD efforts are to:

1. Increase the level of trust and support among organizational members.

2. Increase the incidence of confronting organizational problems, both within groups and among groups in contrast to "sweeping problems under the rug."
3. Create an environment in which the authority of an assigned role is augmented by personal authority based on expertise and knowledge.
4. Increase the openness of communications laterally, vertically, and diagonally.
5. Increase the level of personal enthusiasm and satisfaction in the organization.
6. Find synergistic solutions to problems with greater frequency. [*Synergistic* means the action of two or more organisms to achieve an effect of which each is individually incapable.]
7. Increase the level of self—and group—responsibility in planning and implementation.[4]

The key to the OD process is the *shared approach:* the organization looks at itself and tries to build on its strengths and overcome its weaknesses. This shared approach synthesizes three methods for effecting positive organization change: research, consulting, training. Someone, perhaps an outside consultant, serves as a catalyst, an agent of change, in helping the organization's members build on strengths and overcome problem areas.

There are, of course, other ways of changing an organization. For instance, top management may make a unilateral decision to reorganize the firm or it may launch a supervisory training program. But OD differs from these approaches in at least five ways. First, it uses a research data-gathering feedback model (we will make this clearer in the case that follows) to diagnose and effect needed change. Second, as mentioned, OD is a shared approach. The consultant or other change agent is merely a catalyst, and many levels of management become involved in the process. Third, OD assesses the two causal variables of managerial behavior and organization structure in order to determine whether changes are needed to improve end-results. Fourth, OD is not a one-shot effort. When it is successful, it becomes a continuing part of the organization's way of functioning. Finally, OD is generally most useful when an organization needs to shift to a more participative, open-management system.

THE FOUR PHASES OF AN ORGANIZATION-DEVELOPMENT EFFORT

Different writers have identified different phases of organization-development work.[5] Here we will form four phases: (1) gaining top management support, (2) research and diagnosis, (3) action planning and implementation, and (4) evaluation. These phases overlap and are interrelated, of course, and evaluation is not only the last phase in the sequence but also the first phase in a new cycle.

First Phase—Gaining Top Management Support

This stage begins when a top manager realizes the organization has problems—bad "end-results variables" such as unsatisfactory profits, sales, productivity, and personnel turnover or less tangible variables such as low morale, excessive interdepartmental conflict, and general uneasiness about management's performance. Thus, alerted, the manager turns to someone he thinks can help: an outside consulting firm or management expert or an inside training or personnel director. (Usually, however, an outsider can accomplish much more than an equally competent insider, especially in the first OD cycle.) It is essential that this person develop the trust and confidence of the chief executive. He must also sell top management on the necessity of using a shared approach with other key people in phase 2 (research and diagnosis) and phase 3 (action planning and implementation).

Second Phase—Research and Diagnosis

Psychologist Frank McMahon, Jr., points out that if we really want to know a person, the first step is to ask him directly. Psychologists have allowed this idea to go by the wayside, he believes, and they are afraid to relinquish their positions of omnipotence by soliciting the aid of others in understanding man.[6]

The same criticism is true of consultants trying to diagnose organizational ills. OD consultant Edgar Schein observes that one popular model of consultation is that of doctor-patient: "One or more executives in the organization decide to bring in a consultant or team of consultants to 'look them over,' much as a patient might go to his doctor for an annual physical. The consultants are supposed to find out what is wrong with which part of the organization, and then, like a physician, recommend a program of therapy."[7] This model, he points out, is fraught with difficulties, for a meaningful OD effort solicits the assistance of key members of the organization in research and diagnosis. For example, managers at various levels may be asked to help identify the organization's strengths and weaknesses and to help develop remedies. Obviously, a key assumption of this phase is that top management is often unaware of salient problems or that it needs help in identifying them.

In this research phase, the consultant may interview key people, all of whom should have been briefed on the purpose of the OD effort. The interviews themselves should be conducted in a straightforward way, and each interviewee assured that his information would be included in the overall tabulation, though he would not be identified with a specific input.

Unless the consultant wants to explore a specific area, he usually needs to ask only two questions in order to get enough information for management to work with: (1) What are the strengths of this company? What does it really have going for it? (2) What major problems prevent it from achieving its potential?

Third Phase—Action Planning and Implementation

This phase is also a shared approach. Managers from different levels work with the information derived and develop programs to build on strengths and overcome weaknesses. Invariably the research phase has revealed that most problems are in leadership and motivation, communication and conflict between prople and departments, group problem solving and decision making, and organization structure.

A major assumption is that since there is a shared approach in phases 2 and 3, there is more commitment in implementing recommendations derived from phase 2. As Richard Beckhard has stated, "people support what they help create."[8]

Fourth Phase—Evaluation

This vital phase is sometimes slighted in organization-development efforts. In our experience, this phase should be conducted six months to a year after the start of the OD program. The phase is vital, first, because it gives management feedback on whether the OD program is successful and, second, it helps diagnose why management is failing or surpassing its goals.

A good way to conduct the evaluation is to use the technique of the research and diagnosis phase. If interviews were used in that phase, for example, they should be used again here, and the same questions asked, so that results can be compared. Questionnaires can also measure before-and-after changes in the causal variables of managerial behavior and the intervening variables of motivation, morale, communication, and decision making. In addition, we have found it useful to assess before-and-after changes in some end-results variables such as turnover and productivity. (A cautionary note is that sometimes it is difficult to determine whether changes in end results were caused by outside forces or by the OD program.) In the end, it is to be hoped, a successful OD effort will show positive changes in causal, intervening, and end-result variables, and so lead to an improved state of development for the organization.

ORGANIZATION DEVELOPMENT IN ACTION: A CASE STUDY

For several years one of the authors was an OD consultant for a number of organizations. One particular effort, begun in 1967, was a success, but later experience showed it had several errors. See if you can spot them.

The case was a medium-sized, growing chemical company with headquarters in the West, with branch plants throughout the U.S. It hired numerous engineers and scientists, many with advanced degrees. One plant located in the Mid-South was eighteen months old and involved in a highly technical production process that only one other American company had perfected. Figure 23 shows this local plant's organization. The dotted lines from the plant manager to the two people on each side of him—the manager of industrial relations and the manager of plant accounting—show only that they are physically located in the plant, but that they really report to the vice-president of industrial relations and to the comptroller in the home office.

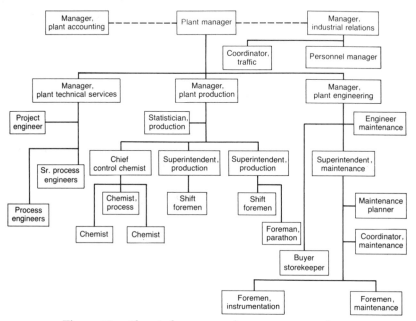

Figure 23.   Chemical company plant organization chart.

After a year and a half, the plant had not perfected its production process, and the plant manager was afraid the plant might close if it did not become profitable within a year. He believed the plant had the expertise to perfect the process but that numerous human problems were hindering it, and so he contacted headquarters about hiring an outside consultant. Eventually the author met with the plant manager, the manager of industrial relations, and an executive from headquarters. They stated they wanted training and development programs for plant employees, especially the top management group, who could best benefit, they felt, with a behavioral-science seminar allowing considerable participation by the managers attending. One problem in the plant, they agreed, was in leadership styles of several key managers. These managers, chosen for their technical expertise, which was critically needed to perfect the production process, had not jelled as a team.

The author interviewed managers participating in the program on their views of plant problems. These interviews, he felt, would broaden the diagnosis, provide information for action planning, and allow the development program to help the plant build on its strengths and overcome its weaknesses. Interviews with nine managers revealed five problem areas (responses are by five to eight managers, as noted):

1. Conflicts between the three departments *(six managers)*
   a. There are conflicts between Production and Technical Services, Production and Engineering, and even Technical Services and Engineering.
   b. Several managers are too critical of other departments and seem unable to visualize other managers' problems.
   c. There are conflicts between departments. Managers just do not work together as a team.
   d. Interdepartmental friction exists; however, much of this goes back to the newness of the plant.
   e. The problem between Technical Services and Production is perhaps traceable to lack of definitions of responsibility and authority.
   f. The biggest problem is conflicts between departments. Major conflict is between the three different department heads.
2. Lack of communication *(eight managers)*
   a. Several managers are weak in communications.
   b. Though they make decisions affecting various people, they do not communicate the decision to all people affected.
   c. They make decisions affecting two departments, but communicate the decisions to only one department.
   d. Communications should receive prime attention. Two different groups should not have to chase down the same avenue for the same answer, with neither group aware of what the other is doing.
3. Faulty interpersonal relations *(six managers)*
   a. Several managers have problems in human relations.
   b. There are poor interpersonal relations between people of the same level up and down the hierarchy.
   c. There is more than usual friction between people— e.g., old guard versus new people.
   d. Some managers are overly critical of other peoples' weaknesses.

e. Managers need to help people of different tempera-
ments and personalities work together.
4. Lack of leadership—or inability to work with and through
subordinates *(six managers)*
a. Several managers have a tendency to solve the problem
for their men.
b. Several managers are somewhat authoritarian in working with their men.
c. One manager is too involved with details and loses
sight of important things.
d. Some are ineffective in working with subordinates.
5. Ineffective implementing of organizing function *(five
managers)*
a. There is fuzziness in assignment of responsibility and
authority; top management is not sure of limits of responsibility and authority.
b. Some people do not fit jobs; managers are covering
part of their jobs and of someone else's job.
c. There is a great need for authority, to spell out relationships of responsibility.
d. One manager tends to bypass chain of command in
dealing with people at lower levels.
6. Other—All interviewees felt they needed training in
performance evaluation of subordinates and were interested in exploring joint target-setting.

The action plans and actions were as follows. First, the interview results were fed back to the plant manager and industrial
relations manager; with the help of the consultant, a training
program for the top group was planned. This program focused on
leadership and motivation, communication and interpersonal
relations, and team building. Second, because the plant manager
wanted to explore utilizing joint-target setting with key subordinates, this topic was included in the tailored program. Third,
the interview results and tentative training program were presented to the managers for their response. Their feedback initiated
minor modifications, and so the training program was initiated.
Finally, at a separate meeting, the plant manager and the three key
department heads decided to have the consultant conduct research to assess the leadership styles of this top group.

Some problems revealed in the plant resulted from ineffective leadership styles, according to some managers. Thus, the consultant suggested a confidential feedback to the four managers regarding their leadership styles. In this strategy, each key manager's superior, peers, and subordinates was asked to indicate strengths and corrective criticisms of how he carried out his duties.

Concurrently with the training program, the interviews were conducted and the results fed back to the four top managers. The four were also allowed to counsel with the consultant regarding the results.

This strategy is not always appropriate, but it helped make this OD program successful. Since all managers were deficient in their operations, the interviews and counseling made them receptive to the training program. The feedback from the interviews also helped three managers start to modify the way they operated as managers, and interviews a year later revealed they had positively modified their leadership styles. One manager who was top-rated by his subordinates was found to be overaggressive, arbitrary, and a cause of excessive interdepartmental conflict in dealing with his peers. A year later comments from peers were almost entirely positive, and all noted an improvement in working relationships.

Prior to the evaluation phase, there were additional actions. First, a tailored training program was implemented for all lower level supervisors. Second, leadership styles were assessed for middle-level managers, and they were provided confidential feedback and counseling. Third, joint-target setting had been implemented with all managers and engineers, with the exception of the shift production foremen. Fourth, to gain greater insight into working with people, the manager of technical services attended sensitivity training.

A year after the program's beginning, the plant was well beyond the break-even point. Quality was improved, production increased, and costs down. The consensus was that OD helped the plant achieve these results.

How did the program measure up? One manager indicated these four general observations about its strengths:

1. Plant has made tremendous strides and steady progress; however, there is still room for improvement.

2. The top management group has developed as managers and functions well as a team.
3. Joint target-setting has been a real asset.
4. Plant manager and production manager work extremely well together and are two of the best managers around.

He also indicated some weaknesses:

1. From a worm's eye view, the entire home office needs reorganizing. For example, home office central engineering and research seems to be almost total confusion. The plant manager and the manager of technical services are subjected to much pressure from the above group, who don't know the process here at all.
2. In our plant a basic problem is the need to upgrade the skills of maintenance mechanics.

A comparison of the interview results before and after the OD program showed that the problems had been or were being resolved, but that now the major problems were different—that is, relationships with the home office needed to be improved and that the maintenance department needed development. The next OD cycle, therefore, focused on these areas, and by any criteria, the plant was well on its way toward achieving the objectives of organization development.

WHAT MAKES ORGANIZATION DEVELOPMENT SUCCESSFUL

Ideally, the outside consultant or change agent should be worked out of his job, for this means the organization is committed to the OD process and builds it into its regular way of operating—that is, it continues to strive for improvement under its own initiative and with its own resources.

The question has been asked, "If OD is so promising, why are not more groups or organizations practicing it?" One expert gives three reasons: "First, individuals have only started to learn within the last twenty years how to create the process of change and growth within their own organizations. Before this, change was something that happened to them. OD is an attempt to integrate what we have learned in this area, and is a very recent idea. Another reason is that OD is a complex process and requires considerable time to spread throughout a total organization. Finally, OD has not always been an irrefutable success. People and organizations are still learning about OD."[9]

One study as to why some OD approaches are successful and others are not concludes that in successful cases the evolution of change demonstrates eight characteristics:

1. The organization, and especially top management, is under considerable external and internal pressure for improvement long before an explicit organization change is contemplated. Performance and/or morale is low. Top management seems to be groping for a solution to its problem.
2. A new man, known for his ability to introduce improvements, enters the organization, either as the official head of the organization, or as a consultant who deals directly with the head of the organization.
3. An initial act of the new man is to encourage a reexamination of past practices and current problems within the organization.
4. The head of the organization and his immediate subordinates assume a direct and highly involved role in conducting this reexamination.
5. The new man, with top management support, engages several levels of the organization in collaborative, fact-finding, problem-solving discussions to identify and diagnose current organization problems.
6. The new man provides others with new ideas and methods for developing solutions to problems, again at many levels of the organization.
7. The solutions and decisions are developed, tested, and found credible for solving problems on a small scale before an attempt is made to widen the scope of change to larger problems and the entire organization.
8. Then change effort spreads with each success experience, and as management support grows, it is gradually absorbed permanently into the organization's way of life.[10]

The concept of OD as we presented it shows most of these characteristics. Moreover, when successfully applied, OD enables an organization to beat the Peter Principle by removing obstacles to individual and organizational development and renewal.

THE SYSTEMS APPROACH

The way we will use the systems approach implies "a way of thinking," as one writer put it,[11] a framework that will allow individuals and organizations to be flexible, adaptable, and creative in reacting to a changing world. We will focus primarily on the value of the concept to the manager and the organization, and will discuss general systems theory only when necessary to explain the systems approach. Systems design and analysis and their associated tools will be described only if they help us better understand the systems concept in the practice of management.

What is a system? One definition that has gained acceptance is "a system is an organized or complex whole; an assemblage or combination of things, or parts forming a complex or unitary whole."[12]

It can be stated that every system has certain characteristics and that most systems should have the following characteristics:

1. A system should have a *purpose*.
2. A system should have *components* . . .
3. A system should have *inputs* and *outputs* . . .
4. A system should have *communication links* . . . They are for the transmission of information in the system, and some or all of them may provide *feedback* for controlling the system.
5. A system should have a *function*. The components individually and/or collectively perform certain functions directed toward the goal.
6. A system should have *procedures*.[13]

Certainly the above characteristics apply to the individual as a system and to the organization. Actually, the *components* of both the individual and the organization are *subsystems*, and likewise the individual is part of a larger organization, and that organization is part of a larger economic, political, and social system. From a systems viewpoint, then, an individual may be viewed on one level as a complete system; on another level a business organization may be viewed as a complete, integrated decision-making system designed to achieve certain objectives; on still another level both the individual and the business organization are subsystems of a larger system—the economic, social, and political environment within which both operate.[14]

Open and Closed Systems

Systems can be considered either closed or open. A closed system tends to move toward a static equilibrium; for example, a heat pump. An open system, such as an organization, on the other hand, "is in a dynamic relationship with its environment and received various inputs, transforms these inputs in some way, and exports outputs."[15] The receipt of inputs in the form of material, energy, and information along with feedback regarding outputs allows the open system to offset the process of decline. Moreover, the open system adapts to its environment by changing processes of its internal components or structure as the need arises.[16] For example, an organization adds people and modifies its organization based on increased demand and sale of its products and services.

Let us now shift gears slightly and think of closed and open systems from a systems approach or a state of mind. All of us are familiar with individuals who deserve the label "closed minded." Closed-minded people have difficulty coping with the changes that are occurring in our society. Change is probably the most critical factor affecting the lives of individuals as well as the operations of a business enterprise; those that can adapt to it survive; those that cannot stagnate and suffer and may even die.

The Business Organization as a System

The systems approach to management has three goals: (1) to define relationships both internal and external to the business organization; (2) to see the pattern of these relationships; and (3) to see the overall purpose of the relationships. As we stated, the systems approach is essentially a way of thinking about the organization—its goals, objectives, and purposes—and the relationships between its parts.

The concept of the business organization as a system is not new, of course. Many successful businessmen have shown the overview and the insight that is now called the systems concept. As one writer states, "If we dig into the history of many of the great builders of our giant corporations—from Theodore Vail of AT & T to Alfred Sloan of General Motors, and any other outstanding architects of corporate management—we will find that these business leaders had the ability to view the business as an integrated whole, that is as a system. They were able to identify strengths and weaknesses and to see how these defined the factors that were critical for success. This approach was the core of their genius for organizing the business and developing its management capabilities."[17]

On the other hand, many of the 100 largest corporations in 1900 are not around today because their management ignored the systems concept. We recall a manufacturing company that moved South to avoid labor unions. The family-owned concern had been producing quality products for several generations; yet within two decades after moving South, it was nearly bankrupt and was forced to sell to a larger corporation. The reasons for the decline were not in the quality of the product but rather in an obsolete and inefficient marketing system and a closed-minded top management that would not accept suggestions for improvement from lower-level managers and professionals.

Writer Robert L. Katz defines three general skills required by a manager—technical, human, and conceptual.[18] Human skills are needed at all levels of management, technical skills are more important at the lower levels, and conceptual skills become increasingly important toward the top. Technical skill involves on-the-job proficiency and the knowledge of products, processes, equipment, and so forth, applicable to that particular position. Conceptual skill is the ability to see the whole picture—the relationships between the parts of the system and the relationships between the organization and systems such as the market, the community, the economy.

The supervisor is concerned with only one system—the rest of the company—but if he can see that system clearly, he is in a better position to define his job in light of the overall objectives of the company. He will more clearly understand the objectives of his department or production line and the policies and procedures of higher levels of management that pertain to him and his function. On the other hand, as we have seen, top management must be able to see the big picture—to take a systems approach. Today, more than ever before, automation, computerization, and the tremendous changes occurring in society have created the requirement of a systems point of view in managing a company. Systems thinking on the part of top management can protect a company from the same type of fate which caused the buggy manufacturer to go bankrupt.

SUMMARY

In this chapter we have taken a systems point of view and introduced you to the concept of organization development. Although OD cannot do everything, it does show promise as a conceptual framework for integrating our ideas about change and also serves as an action-oriented approach to help organizations move from one state to an improved state of development.

QUESTIONS

1. Do you agree or disagree with the assertion that organization development is merely the improvement of overall organization efficiency and effectiveness through the systematic and pervasive application of theory Y, enlightened management concepts, and the systems approach to management?

2. How could an OD approach be used to convert a highly structured system with an autocratic style of management to a more open system with a participative style of management? The change is believed to be necessary because of both internal and external pressure. Employee morale is low and profits have declined substantially during the past year.

3. In nearly any conversation concerning the systems approach, two questions always seem to arise. First, is the systems approach anything new, or is it just a new term applied to old methods of managing an enterprise? Second, is the systems approach merely a theoretical approach or is it really something that can be used in the practical application of business management? Discuss.

4. From a systems viewpoint, if an organization becomes too open or too closed, what are the probable consequences? How might an organization prevent such a state of affairs?

NOTES

1. Paul R. Lawrence and Joy W. Lorsch, *Developing Organizations: Diagnosis and Action* (Reading, Mass.: Addison-Wesley Publishing Company, 1969), pp. 9–10.

2. Rensis Likert, *The Human Organization* (New York: McGraw-Hill Book Company, 1967), pp. 26–29.

3. Wendell L. French, "Organization Development: What It Is and Is Not," *The Personnel Administrator*, January-February, 1971, p. 4.

4. *Ibid.*, p. 6.

5. Richard Beckhard, in *Organization Development: Strategies and Models* (Reading, Mass.: Addison-Wesley Publishing Company, 1969), p. 9, pinpointed five phases of organization-wide change efforts: (1) diagnosis, (2) strategy planning, (3) education, (4) consulting and training, and (5) evaluation. One of the authors, Donald Mosely, in "A Tailored Approach to Management Development," *Management Decision*, Spring, 1970, has also identified four phases: (1) gaining top management support, (2) research and consulting, (3) program formulation and implementation, and (4) assessment of results. Lawrence and Lorsch in *Developing Organizations*, pp. 20–21, have identified four phases: (1) diagnosis, (2) action planning, (3) implementation, and (4) evaluation. All three approaches basically describe the same process. In this book we will integrate the phases of Lawrence and Lorsch.

6. Frank B. McMahon, Jr., "Psychological Testing—A Smoke Screen Against Logic," *Psychology Today*, January, 1969, p. 55.

7. Edgar H . Schein, *Process Consultation: Its Role in Organization Development* (Reading, Mass.: Addison-Wesley Publishing Company, 1969), p. 6.

8. Beckhard, *Organization Development*, p. 27.

9. Lyman K. Randall, "Common Questions and Tentative Answers Regarding Organization Development," *California Management Review*, Spring, 1971, pp. 49–50.

10. Larry E. Greiner, "Patterns of Organization Change," *Harvard Business Review*, May-June, 1967, pp. 122–23.

11. Donald L. Caruth, "The Total Systems Concept," *Business Studies*, Fall, 1968, p. 71.

12. Richard Johnson, Fremont Kast, and James Rosensweig, *The Theory and Management of Systems* (New York: McGraw-Hill Book Company, 1963), p. 4.

13. Richard B. Kershner, "A Survey of Systems Engineering Tools and Techniques" in Charles D. Flagle, William H. Huggins, and Robert H. Roy, eds., *Operation Research and Systems Engineering* (Baltimore: Johns Hopkins Press, 1960), p. 141.

14. Robert J. Mockler, "The Systems Approach to Business Organizations," *California Management Review*, Winter, 1968, pp. 53–57.

15. Fremont E. Kast and James E. Rosenzweig, *Organization and Management: A Systems Approach* (New York: McGraw-Hill Book Company, 1969), pp. 118–19.

16. *Ibid.*

17. Allen Harvey, "Systems Can *Too* Be Practical," *Business Horizons*, Summer, 1964, p. 63.

18. Robert L. Katz, "Skills of an Effective Administrator," *Harvard Business Review*, January-February, 1955, pp. 33–42.

13

Management in the Future: Decentralization and Participative Management

In this final chapter we will speculate about the future—how various trends and changes will affect human organizations and how managers at all levels will operate in working with and through people. In this view from the top, we will try to identify the difficulties, challenges, and opportunities that higher level managers face, so that the operative manager will have an appreciation for top management's role, can do a better job in his present position, and finally be better able to plan his career goals.

DECENTRALIZATION VERSUS CENTRALIZATION

Early in the book we examined the concept of delegation. Real insight and skill in delegating without stifling initiative and without losing control are essential for any operative manager. Closely related is decentralization versus centralization. Top management will have to make decisions regarding centralization versus decentralization that will affect the destiny of future organizations.

Of course, no organization is completely centralized or decentralized; it is a relative concept. The concept of decentralization, like the concept of delegation, has to do with the degree to which authority is dispersed. However, where delegation usually refers to the extent to which an individual manager delegates authority and responsibility to people reporting to him, decentralization is a broader concept and refers to the extent top management delegates authority from one organization unit or level to another.

Another way of looking at it, and the definition we prefer, is that decentralization means "shifting 'downward' the point at which all the employees necessary to do a complete job come together and report to a common supervisor."[1] Drawing from this definition, writers Strauss and Sayles point out the advantages and disadvantages of decentralization:

Advantages

1. It means more responsibility can be delegated to the supervisors and managers.
2. The organization structure will be built around the flow of work, therefore allowing the large company to enjoy the human relations advantages of the small company.
3. All operations that need to be integrated come under a common supervisor at the lowest possible level.
4. Managers and workers who must coordinate their activities are made members of the same team, which, of course improves communications.

Disadvantages

1. Decentralization requires unusually able personnel managers and employees who can accept delegation and general supervision and the responsibilities these entail.
2. It demands that all managers in the company share a common understanding of the methods, policies, and objectives of the organization.
3. Many organizations are composed of parts that are too interdependent to allow for a great deal of autonomy.
4. Finally, in some organizations that have undergone decentralization, duplication of functions and efforts can become a problem.[2]

In general, a firm following a policy of decentralization would allow operative managers to better practice the concepts and principles in this book. Certainly we can say that morale is usually found to be higher in decentralized companies. On the other hand, some companies have gotten into difficulties by shifting to decentralization primarily because top management lost control of their decentralized operations. What trend does the future hold for business organizations, decentralization or centralization?

In 1958 management theorists Harold Leavitt and Thomas L. Whisler published an article entitled "Management in the 1980s," which caused shock waves in the business world. They predicted that by the 1980s large organizations would have gone through a process of recentralization and that the trend toward participative management would be reversed, except for top managers working with other top managers and specialists. They also predicted that most middle management jobs would become highly structured and routinized, with the majority of middle jobs moving downward in status and pay.

They based their predictions on the increasing use of the computer and what they called *information technology,* which they defined as being composed of three related parts: "One includes techniques for processing large amounts of information rapidly, and it is epitomized by the high-speed computer. A second part centers around the application of statistical and mathematical methods to decision-making problems; it is represented by techniques like mathematical programing, and by methodologies like operations research. A third part is in the offing, though its applications have not yet emerged very clearly; it consists of the simulation of higher-order thinking through computer programs."[3] They went on to say that because information technology and the computer makes centralization much easier, management would probably revert to it, for in their judgment decentralization had been negatively motivated—that is prior to the high-speed computer, management had to decentralize to keep up with the increasing size of firms and complexity of technology. Information technology would also, they believed, allow higher management to reduce the number of middle managers, and those left would not so much manage as be routine technicians who would have to satisfy higher level needs off the job.[4]

If Leavitt and Whisler are correct, then this book is already

obsolete or soon will be. However, we take exception to their conclusions. In the decade and a half since their article some trends
are discernible. Information technology has indeed given top management the ability to shift to a highly centralized way of operating.
But it has also provided them with the ability to shift toward more
decentralization and more participative management—and with
less likelihood of top management losing control. Support for this
view is made by writer Max Ways in a 1966 article: "It is easy to
think of examples where authority now dispersed might be efficiently reconcentrated at the top with the aid of computers. But
such reconcentration is not the main trend in organization today.
Since the new information technology began coming into use in the
fifties, the trend toward decentralization has probably been accel-
erated, indicating that there were better reasons for decentralization than the lack of instant information at headquarters. Computers can be used to reinforce either a centralizing policy or its
opposite; the probability increases that decentralization will in
the coming decades be carried to lengths undreamed of ten years
ago."[5]

Ways also wrote that in the U.S. the trend in management was
toward organizations based on theory Y assumptions rather than
theory X. As a result, organization structures were changing so
that operative managers had opportunities to exercise more self-
control and to participate in goal-setting, both for the organization
and for themselves. Moreover, he felt, the opportunities were
increasing for higher level need satisfaction on the job.

MANAGEMENT AND CHANGE

To the old saying that nothing is certain but death and taxes, we
would add a third word: change. In the past few decades the world
has undergone changes at perhaps a faster pace than ever before in
the history of mankind. Such changes are especially significant for
managers, when we consider trends in education, job opportunities, and values and attitudes. Let us examine these three areas
and see if they support our contention that enlightened and participative management is the wave of the future.

Education.   The population of the United States is becoming
better educated than the citizens of any country in the history of

the world. In 1975 probably one out of every four employees has a university degree, whereas a few years ago it was only one in ten. Less than a decade ago it was rare to find someone in business with a graduate degree; today it is commonplace. Community colleges and vocational technical institutes are producing graduates at rapid rate. The rise in adult education programs represents a trend in which people are becoming reeducated at different times throughout their lives. It is a well known fact that the more people are educated the more they expect in the way of enlightened and participative management.

Job Opportunities. The increasing demand for managerial, professional, technical, skilled, clerical and service workers is coupled with a reduction in oportunities for unskilled workers. The demand for laborers, for example, is "expected to change little between 1968 and 1980 in spite of the rise in manufacturing and construction which employ most laborers."[6] However, the demand for skilled workers (who consist of one out of every five male workers) is expected to jump to 12.2 million by 1980—a gain of 2.2 million over 1968. These are jobs that "offer the opportunity to create with the hands—to produce, to build, to breathe life back into a seemingly hopeless maze of wire and disabled electrical gear."[7] These jobs are not highly structured, routine tasks: they are creative and challenging, and the same is true for most other expanding job-opportunity areas. As we have seen, supervising such works and employees calls for more enlightened management.

Values and Attitudes. Society has spawned numerous legislation that affects business, but probably the greatest single influence has been the changing values and attitudes of the young people of America. The youth of America seem to be less interested in purely materialistic goals and more interested in finding meaning and purpose in life. One article stated "that fully 40 percent of the nation's college students can be included in a group characterized by a notable 'lack of concern for money' making."[8] This does not mean young people are not interested in business careers, but rather that they expect more from the corporation than just profit and service-oriented goals. They expect business to adopt a broader set of social values and managers to utilize the corporation as a vehicle for effecting positive change to enrich society not only economically but socially and morally. Already professional managers are embracing a broader set of social responsibilities, from doing something about pollution and discrimination to creating a work environment where their employees can find more fulfillment.

Other changes, of course, are also taking place which will cause organizations to become more adaptive to human values— affluence, leisure, urbanization, the civil and human rights movements, and international business developments. The trend, we believe, is toward the system concept, decentralization, and enlightened management. Thus, operative managers in the future will have a demanding and increasingly important role. Both individual and group participation will be the key to providing a meaningful work situation for employees, and the operative manager will be the prime motivating force. He will also need to guide the efforts of the bulk of employees, maintain clear communication lines, reduce distortion from the communication network, translate higher objectives and advise on setting specific targets at lower levels that meet with the overall objectives. He will be part of the big picture and concerned with achieving goals and maintaining a healthy psychological climate.

We may conclude by quoting management professor John Mee, who in skillful broad strokes has portrayed the organization of the future as it now appears it will become in reality:

> As organization evolves toward the systems concept, management leadership will shift from a role of autocratic and centralized decision making to one of support and linkage with decentralized decisions and planning in order to achieve specific quantifiable, and realistic systems results and rational goals. Many individuals within the organization will thereby be able to realize satisfaction from their contributions in contrast to a few managers in organizations built around a pyramid system of authority.
>
> In systems of organization built around a results management concept, management will be considered a human resource and authority will flow from the desired results of a system rather than from the dictation of one individual. The knowledge, skills, and values of individuals will determine their place in the order of subsystem and the total

system. Their contribution and their opportunities for achievement and self-realization will be judged by their competence to achieve desired results in systems assignments instead of by the ownership of birthrights, land, or financial capital.[9]

QUESTIONS

1. Speculate and write your own views as to management in the future.
2. Was the building and development of America based on a theory X or theory Y management philosophy? What do you predict for the next thirty years? Support your position.
3. What skills are essential for success in lower and middle management positions? Are additional skills needed to succeed in top management positions? Why or why not?

NOTES

1. George Strauss and Leonard Sayles, *Personnel: The Human Problems of Management*, rev. ed. (Englewood Cliffs, N.J.: Prentice-Hall, 1967), p. 414.
2. *Ibid.*, pp. 414–15.
3. Harold Leavitt and Thomas L. Whisler, "Management in the 1980s," *Harvard Business Review*, November-December 1958, pp. 41–48.
4. *Ibid.*, pp. 42–46.
5. Max Ways, "Tomorrow's Management," *Fortune*, July 1, 1966, p. 1.
6. U.S. Department of Labor, *Occupational Outlooks Handbook*, 1970–71 edition, Bureau of Labor Statistics, Bulletin No. 1650, p. 17.
7. *Occupational Outlook Quarterly*, "The Crafts," U.S. Department of Labor, Spring, 1971.
8. Leslie M. Lawson, "The Human Concept: New Philosophy for Business," *Business Horizons*, December, 1969, p. 29.
9. John Mee, "Speculation About Human Organization in the 21st Century," *Business Horizons*, February, 1971, p. 16.

Appendix

Cases and Role-Playing Situations

The purpose of this appendix is to give you the opportunity to practice the art of management by attempting to deal with problems and situations confronting managers in the business world. Because learning is more effective when it is an active rather than passive process, the cases and role-playing situations allow you to apply the theory and concepts in the text in a real-world context.

In using the role-playing situations, we suggest the following guidelines: First, the role-players should be given the opportunity to study their roles and the general situations in advance before role-playing action begins. Second, the role-players are not limited to the brief description of the role, but may introduce new thoughts and ideas as long as they meet the test of realism and stay within the context of the general situation. Third, it should be kept in mind that many times we learn more from failure than from success. Finally, those who are not role-players should serve as observers and participate with the role-players in a disciplined reflection regarding the experience.

Some questions that might be examined are: Was the problem dealt with effectively? What happened that was helpful? What was unhelpful? How could we do it better next time in a similar situation? Are there any generalized principles we can draw from this experience that might help in future situations?

CASES FOR PART 1

Case 1—The Growing Organization

Assume you will be graduating from college and will be hired as personnel manager and accountant for Markham Lumber Company in Birmingham, Alabama. This company has relied on its owner and president, Mr. Markham, quite heavily. He is an outstanding salesman, but admits to knowing little about organization and management. As Figure 24 shows, the company has grown

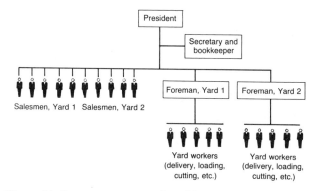

Figure 24. Present structure of Markham Lumber Company.

gradually to the present number of employees. The president has hired you because you have worked for the company two consecutive summers, once as a yard worker and once as a salesman. Therefore, you are very familiar with the company and most of the men. Second, since you are an accounting major with a minor in management, he wants you to develop an accounting procedure for the company as well as suggest a new and better way of setting up the company. Mr. Markham has been too busy to call on some of the major accounts; this is why he wants a better organization setup. He also says that his salesmen are not highly motivated, even though they are on a part-commission basis. There are two lumber yards owned by the company: yard 1 is the major yard and yard 2 is about four miles away. Both yards carry the same line of merchandise, and for the most part salesmen in each yard sell mainly to customers who visit the yard to place their orders or who place their orders by phone. In some cases, salesmen may leave the yard to talk with a customer; however, this is not ordinarily true. Draw up the organization chart you would recommend to Mr. Markham.

Case 2—The Missing Speech

After reading the following telephone exchange between a company president and his public relations director, determine who is responsible for the communications breakdown and why.

> PRESIDENT: Charlie, where's that environmental speech you were going to write for me? I just got back in the office and I at least wanted to look it over before I give it in an hour. Wasn't it supposed to be ready yesterday?
>
> PUBLIC RELATIONS DIRECTOR: Mr. Barrington, I gave the speech situation and facts to Sam, since he knows so much about the environmental movement, and I knew he'd do a good job. I don't know why he hasn't finished it. Want me to call him?
>
> PRESIDENT: Never mind; I'll do it myself. (*Dials.*) Sam, Barrington here. Charlie said you were working up that environment speech.
>
> SAM: Yes, sir, I gave it to Charlie's secretary three days ago to type up. Don't you have it?
>
> PRESIDENT: I do not, and I'm supposed to deliver it in fifty-three minutes.

The handwritten draft of the speech lay in the in-basket of Charlie's secretary who had been out for two days with the flu.

Case 3—The Unsigned Letter

Hanson, the general manager of Ajax Corporation, received an unsigned letter at his central office in Cleveland from an employee in the Ajax plant in Williamsboro. As he read it, he remembered there had been some worry about a union being voted into the Williamsboro plant.

Dear Mr. Hanson:

I and many of the other men here at Williamsboro have worked at Ajax for a long time, and since Ajax has always treated us right, I want to let you know about some things I think you don't know about. Several good men have left Ajax recently. It's because some management people here are only out for themselves and don't really care about the company. Ask any production foreman, and he will know what I'm talking about. Unless something is done soon, a lot of other good people will leave too. I am writing you this letter because I like it here and don't want to have to leave. Please don't think this is only a person out to get somebody. I really think you don't know what the situation is here, and I wanted to let you know.

The chain of command between Hanson and workers at the Williamsboro plant is shown in Figure 25. What action should Hanson take?

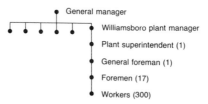

General manager

Williamsboro plant manager

Plant superintendent (1)

General foreman (1)

Foremen (17)

Workers (300)

Figure 25. Chain of command between General Manager and Williamsboro plant.

Case 4—Line-Staff Dispute

PRODUCTION FOREMAN: What a job! I've got top management breathing down my neck to get the work out. My men do a real good job, considering the equipment and space and conditions around here. Sometimes the pressure gets to me and I push the men a little too hard, and they get peeved at me. Then I've got trouble with Maintenance. You ask them to repair something and sometimes it's days before they do anything. They give you this runaround about how much work they've got to do, but I know other departments get what they need right away. You tell me how to get a job done when you've got to depend on somebody like that. I've blown off about it to the superintendent, but nothing seems to happen.

MAINTENANCE FOREMAN: This job! I've got foremen running around saying they've got to have this and that right away. So try to assign some priorities to the jobs and some guy will take it to the superintendent. What really burns is they put pressure on my men to get a job out fast and not worry about how they do it. You try to do what's right, and some guys say you play favorites. I'd like anybody to show me a better way to operate with the small staff I've got.

What is the major problem here and what can be done about it? Role-play the parts of the two foremen.

Case 5—Southland Flying Club

The club has 310 members with ten selected to serve on the policy-making board of directors. The board elects one member to serve as President without pay. Six members are elected (by the total membership) to form the Flying Committee and six are also elected to form the Social Committee.

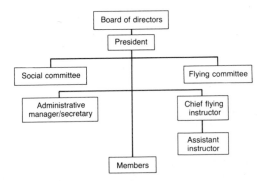

Figure 26. Organization of the Southland Flying Club.

The board of directors employs the Chief Flying Instructor and his three assistants, all highly trained aviation specialists, and the Administrative Manager/Secretary, a trained accountant who is employed full time.

The President, directors, and other committee members are primarily businessmen, who know little about aviation other than how to fly. However, they control the permanent staff without attempting to understand the day-to-day running of the organization. They also have a tendency to become upset when the permanent staff use their initiative in these matters. One problem in particular is that many people give the permanent staff orders and instructions, and sometimes the different orders conflict.

Assume you are the Chief Flying Instructor. What should you do to correct this situation? Role-play the case.

CASES FOR PART 2

Case 6—The Unmotivated Employee

White works just enough to keep the foreman off his back. "Why kill myself?" he says. "The job's dirty, the pay's bad, so why do more than I have to?"

What would you recommend to the foreman to try to change White's attitude?

Case 7—The Foreman's Problem

The foreman of an assembling department finds that when he gives his workers instructions, they seem to understand what he says, but when they do the job, it often seems to be loused up. What advice can you offer?

Case 8—The Required Meeting

John Bigham returned from a meeting with other production foremen at which the plant manager announced a new company policy in which every Friday all departments were to have fifteen-minute meetings with all workers present. The purpose of the meetings, which were to last until 5 P.M., the regular quitting time, was to have the foremen make announcements of interest to the workers and answer any questions. Bigham did not know how well he would be able to conduct a meeting with his workers, since he had had little experience with that sort of thing. What if the men started to gripe about working conditions, wages, or the like at the meetings?

Are Bigham's fears justified?

What are the possible advantages and disadvantages of such meetings?

Case 9—The Overheard Conversation

Overheard in the men's rest room of a large company: "Reeding doesn't know what's going on here in his own department, and I'm sure not going to be the one to tell him. He probably wouldn't listen anyway. A lot of the guys have some good ideas if only he'd let them sound off. But you learn fast around here to do as you're told and not bother anybody with ideas about how to make this place better."

What could be some things Reeding does not know about? What does this little incident tell us about Reeding as a leader? Can a superior really know what is going on in his department without placing excessively rigid controls on his workers?

Case 10—Hawthorne Company

An office manager for Hawthorne has a staff with high morale and generally good productivity, but several people have been extending their coffee breaks by five to eight minutes. He feels that the more conscientious workers resent this, yet he wonders whether he should stop these extended breaks and risk alienating those workers. How should he handle this problem?

Another office manager for Hawthorne has an office staff of six girls which has separated into two cliques constantly at each other's throats. The clique of younger workers wears fashionable clothes (shorter skirts, slacks), which the older women resent. The clique of older workers joke about trashy fashions, which irritates the younger women. This is only one of the frictions. At meetings, each person sides with other members in her clique. How can the office manager prevent such cliques from forming? Should he want to prevent all cliques? What can he do about his present problem?

Case 11—The Disadvantaged Worker

John, 23, a black, is from a poor family. Discharged from the army, he gets a job with a manufacturing firm. The foreman gives him fifteen minutes of instructions and tells him to get busy.

Asked if he understands what to do, John says yes.

Thirty minutes later, the foreman returns, notices John has loused up the job, and yells, "I thought that you understood what to do, boy," in front of the other workers. "I'll show you only once more how to do it, and you'd better pay attention, or you're fired!" John gets the work done correctly, he guesses, because the foreman comes around to check several times, but does not tell him anything.

Next day, John does not show up for work. The foreman remarks, "They're all alike. They hate somebody telling them what to do. Just as good we got rid of him so I can find somebody else with a better attitude."

Evaluate the foreman's approach. What would you have done had you been the foreman? To what extent does a foreman have to use an autocratic approach when supervising relatively unskilled employees?

Case 12—The New Manager

Suppose your company has decided to build a branch plant in a small town twenty-five miles south of Montgomery, Alabama. You are moved from your present position of assistant manager in a California plant and promoted to manager of the new plant. The company has assigned you an assistant manager from another California plant. Both you and your assistant manager are responsible for recruiting, selecting, and training both supervisors and operative employees for a new plant.

On May 1, the plant is ready to start operation. Based on past experience, the home office has set quotas for the new plant to reach, and after one year's time expects production to average what other plants normally produce. The other plants around the country average 1000 units a day. The company expects the new plant to be producing 300 units in three months; 500 units in six months; 700 units in nine months; and 1000 units in twelve months.

After nine months in Alabama, the new plant is averaging 860 units per day and you as plant manager feel on top of the world. The new supervisors are well trained, morale is high, and you and the assistant manager are practicing general supervision, letting the supervisors run their own departments and supervising by results.

The next day your assistant manager requests a transfer back to California. He is happy in Alabama, but his wife cannot seem to adjust to the South and is homesick. Realizing the potential of the assistant manager, you check with the home office and grant the transfer request.

The home office sends down a new assistant manager from a Pennsylvania plant. This man has always received good performance ratings and is noted for getting out production. His style of supervision is somewhat different from your own in that he believes in close supervision and really pushing for production.

Much to your dismay, around the 10th of the month production begins leveling off and begins decreasing; by the end of the tenth month, production has dropped to 780 units a day.

Supervisor Jack Jones. You are really upset over the way that new assistant manager keeps sticking his nose in your department. Any time he sees anything that the operative people are doing that he does not like, he goes directly to them and corrects them. He has followed the chain of command only once and that was when he complained about the operative people taking longer than ten minutes for their break. It's a wonder he didn't chew them all out as a group. Your people are getting spooked up and production is dropping off. One of these days you just might tell that guy off and go back to your father-in-law's body shop.

Supervisor Smith. Your two best buddies in the service were from Pennsylvania so you thought you would get along fine with the new assistant manager. Boy, were you wrong. The former assistant manager had high expectations, but you really respected him. He always gave you general instructions about what was expected and then left it up to you and your men to get production out. If something happened and you did not make production, he would ask what happened and what could be done about it. He trusted you and your men, and you responded by having the best producing department in the plant.

This new assistant manager doesn't seem to trust you at all. He is constantly checking up on you and trying to get you to change to the way they did things in the Pennsylvania plant. Last week he chewed you out in front of all your men. Lately you've been sharp of temper at home and on the job. You are thinking about talking to the plant manager about this new assistant manager, since morale and production are on the decrease in your department.

New Assistant Manager. You've always considered yourself capable and conscientious, but this new job is getting you down. These Southern farm boys are not measuring up to your standards, and production has fallen down. Well, you've been in tough situations before and have come through all right. This situation reminds you of the first time you were appointed a supervisor in the plant in Pennsylvania. Most of the men there were former coal miners who were a hard-nosed bunch. They tried to get the upper hand on you, but you were as tough as they were and eventually earned their respect by becoming an expert in every job in the plant and staying on top of things.

In your opinion the trouble has been that these workers have had lax supervision. You notice that in most departments the operators take fifteen to twenty minutes rather than the prescribed ten minutes for a coffee break. Also, many times you've checked on a department and found several of the men talking rather than working. If the manager will back you up, you are going to lay it on the line to the supervisors that production had better start improving or some deadwood will be eliminated.

There is only one thing that bothers you: production was at a pretty high level when you first came and has since dropped. It's your job to get it back up and even higher and come hell or high water you will get it up.

Role-play a meeting between (1) the plant manager and the two supervisors, (2) the two supervisors and the assistant manager, and (3) the plant manager and the assistant manager.

Case 13—Role Playing: Joint Target-Setting

Assume you will play the role of boss and a classmate will play the role of subordinate in a joint target-setting meeting. Each of you should come to class prepared for a joint target-setting conference. Assume that targets will be established for the next six months and that the number of formal check points along the way will also be determined, as well as the means for measuring the extent to which the targets will be accomplished. Your instructor will provide details about the positions held by you and your subordinate and other assumptions about the situation.

Case 14—Role Playing: The President's Dilemma*

Your company endeavors to adapt to the local customs so as to fit into the community it operates in. Because of this policy, the plant has not employed blacks other than as janitors or for other menial jobs. Recently, however, the company received a large government contract which requires that the plant employ at least 25 percent blacks and that no discrimination be shown in job placement. One foreman reported to the personnel department that one of his men came up to him in the plant and said, "I heard that coloreds are going to take over my job. I ain't gonna stand for this and besides, I won't even work beside one of them. Most of the men feel as I do, too."

The above situation has occurred many times in the business world in recent years. Some companies have found solutions to the problem; others have met miserable failure. Try to arrive at a successful solution to the problem for your company. The members of the problem-solving group are as follows: (1) company president and general manager (committee chairman), (2) company attorney, (3) engineering manager, (4) personnel manager, (5) plant superintendent, and (6) director of public relations.

Use the names of the individuals who are playing the assigned roles. In playing the roles, use enthusiasm and portray the individual as given to you in the role assignments given below. You are not entirely limited to the role as written, but it should be the basis for your position. You undoubtedly know people who fit each role; therefore, try to play the role as these people would.

The decision reached by the group should be workable, but each of you has ideas as to what decision you would like to see reached.

Company Attorney. As an attorney you feel that blacks have been discriminated against for over one hundred years. This is an opportunity for the white society to rectify its past wrongs and even repay its social debts to black America. You have been very active in civil rights work in the community and have given free legal aid to its causes. It is your position that regardless of education and training the black man should be given jobs, for it is his cultural and environmental background that has made him the way he is.

* Our thanks to Professor Roy Carpenter of General Motors Institute for allowing us to use this case.

Therefore, no present test can adequately measure blacks' ability on the job. They should be hired regardless of test scores and other selection methods routinely used in hiring. You are to play the role of an active integrationist and present arguments to hire blacks regardless of the short-run effect upon the company. In the long run, you're sure, this decision will be best for the company, community, and society as a whole.

Company President and General Manager (Committee Chairman). Your role is to develop a workable plan for implementing the new hiring policy. You want a plant that will keep the organization stable and committed to its objectives of making a profit and at the same time serve society and its needs. The committee is to aid you in reaching a decision, whether unanimous or not; a decision must be reached. You feel that the group method of solving an issue is a must if people are to accept the adopted policy.

Your role should be one of directing and leading the group to a solution. The outcome of this policy committee meeting could very well mean your success or failure as a manager. Remember, objectivity is your goal. Biases should not enter into this important decision.

Plant Superintendent. You are to represent the company as well as the workers in the plant. The workers have confidence in you and your ability to represent their interests. Recently, many workers in the plant have suspected that a policy of hiring more blacks was coming soon. Therefore, many workers have come to you stating their position. The majority of the workers indicate that they are opposed to hiring blacks because production will decrease, quality will decline, and management will really start to ride herd on manufacturing. Others feel that they may quit if the ratio of blacks to whites exceeds 1 to 10. They say that there are a few good blacks but certainly not enough to justify a greater ratio than this. Remember, these are trained, skilled workers relating these things to you. A few workers say they will work with blacks if they have to, but they are really not enthusiastic about it. Morale is pretty low. Your role is to represent the plant workers and foremen; at the same time you realize that continual work is dependent upon meeting the government's requirement.

Personnel Manager. You are in favor of meeting the government's requirement, because you know that this will get the departments of Labor and Defense off your back. You feel that blacks can be trained to do the job, but that a training program will have to be established to accomplish this end. You feel that no theory yet developed shows any innate difference in ability among the races. Further, part of your job is to hire new workers, and the black work force is plentiful. The white labor force is tight, and you just cannot find an adequate supply of labor among the whites. Your role is to sell management and the committee on utilizing this labor force, for it is your firm belief that there is no difference between the races. Also, you want to initiate the new policy immediately to keep the government from interfering and causing you problems.

Engineering Manager. You feel that blacks are incapable of performing tasks of a technical nature. You feel that blacks may be able to perform operations in the plant but certainly not engineering or office work. You do have reservations even about plant work, but you would rather have this than a black in your area. Most of the blacks you have known are lazy, irresponsible, and in general are not suited for work other than menial tasks. You feel that the Supreme Court and Washington are forcing this down the throats of all Americans and that this is a communist plot to divide the country. You are in all respects a bigot, but you do feel that there are a few good white man's niggers around. You have many logical reasons why blacks will not fit into the industrial world. Your role is to prevent hiring blacks at all costs, for doing so will be the downfall of the country and the free-enterprise system. It is infringing upon the right of private property and you resent any government interference.

Public Relations Director. You realize that the community will balk at the company's policy of hiring 25 percent blacks, if this is the decision made. On the other hand, you're concerned that your competitors will certainly make the company look bad in the public eye if this government contract is revoked for failure to meet the policy. You are quite familiar with the national exposure of many companies who have had contracts rescinded by the government. And you know the NAACP can really make a company look bad when it wants to. Yet there is no doubt that the community is going to be upset if the antidiscrimination policy is followed. Naturally, your main concern with whatever action the company takes is to see to it that adverse publicity is minimized.

CASES FOR PART 3

Case 15—Management Consulting to Woodworking Company

Assume you have been called in as a management consultant to a woodworking company. The company employs slightly over 2000 employees and manufactures cabinets and related items. A mutual investment fund recently appraised the company as being sound technically with a strong capital base. The company has been in the black since 1960 and the profits have increased every year since 1960.

The president of the company in his first conversation with you indicates that despite increasing profits he is unhappy with the company's economic performance. Utilizing financial ratios, cost figures, and sales volume, he makes a strong case that profits should be substantially higher than they have been for the past five years. Although he suspects what some of the reasons are for the lackluster performance, he wants you to study the company's operations, to indicate problem areas, and to recommend solutions.

Your preliminary investigation reveals the following points:

1. Approximately 40 percent of the operative forces are black; however, there are no blacks in supervisory positions.
2. A study of labor turnover for past years indicates excessive turnover of operative employees. Utilizing a company estimate of training cost for a new employee, you estimate the company is losing approximately $500,000 yearly on turnover above the average rate for the industry.
3. The carpenters' union recently won an election. Prior to this election, the company had defeated the union in three previous attempts to organize the employees. You

also note that the company created some ill feeling among operative people in the manner in which it opposed the union. Many of its tactics were branded as unfair labor practices by the National Labor Relations Board.

4. The only type of management development has been a watered-down human-relations course for all levels of management and a supervisory-development course for twenty first-line supervisors. Interviews with the supervisors indicate they thought the program was good; however, they felt their bosses were the ones who needed to attend.

5. The company operates on a twenty-four-hour basis, with three shifts of eight hours each. For the so-called boneyard night shift, operative employees are paid a higher rate than for other shifts.

6. Supervisors who work the night shift are not paid a higher rate. On the other hand, supervisors rotate so that they work only one week out of every eight at night. The net effect is to cause operative people to have a number of different supervisors in the course of a year.

7. Interviews with the bottom two levels of supervisors indicate that a morale problem is developing because outsiders are always brought in to fill openings.

8. No performance evaluation or counseling procedures exist for supervisory and staff people.

9. In your judgment, performance standards for operative employees are adequate.

10. A piecework incentive program, which exists in a number of departments, seems to work effectively.

11. Average wage rates for operative employees are $2.79 an hour. This average is 14¢ above the average of woodworking plants in general. However, the plant is below wage rates of most of the city's manufacturing plants.

12. The chain of command is used to convey information upward and orders downward. (Exceptions are standardized reports going to production control and accounting.)

13. The only meetings between different levels are primarily to convey information downward.

14. The organization environment is highly autocratic, with considerable authoritarian leadership.

15. The company is located in a city of 150,000 people and is faced with a recruiting problem in that there exists a tight labor market.

Since a consulting agreement for a fixed fee was agreed to in advance, time does not permit a more detailed investigation. Based on the above information and inferences from it, write out your report and recommendations to the president of the company.

Case 16—OD Role Playing

Assume you are the OD consultant involved in the chemical plant case described in Chapter 12. If you will recall, it was decided to have the consultant conduct interviews to assess the leadership styles of the top four managers. Each manager was given confidential feedback about the results and provided an opportunity to counsel with you, the consultant, regarding the feedback. The following report represents the feedback to the manager of technical services.

> To: Manager, Plant Technical Services
> From: OD Consultant
> Re: A summary of pro and con comments from six subordinates and peers regarding your style of leadership as Manager of Technical Services.

> This summary is provided so that you may have a better insight into your managerial style and the impact you have on others in implementing your responsibilities as manager.
> You are the only person who will receive a copy of this report. As a result of this confidential report, it is hoped that through self-appraisal you will be able to improve your effectiveness as a manager by building on your strengths and improving your weak points. You will be given an opportunity to counsel with the consultant regarding the results should you desire to.
> A. *Pro*
>   1. Strong in research area.
>   2. Good at handling administrative details and paperwork. Everything that goes through has plenty of paper to justify it.

Con

1. Conversely, loss in time due to excessive paperwork is a weakness. In the opinion of the interviewee, many things cannot be black or white, and on some things the department must simply take a chance.
2. He is not receptive to ideas that do not fit his concept of how to do the job.
3. Seems to be a first-class engineer, but he has to fight himself to give people engineering responsibility.
4. As a manager he should depend on his people instead of doing the work himself.
   a. He is creating a bottleneck because everything must be closely examined by him.
   b. He should rely more on the technical skills of the people under him unless their skills do not measure up to standards.
5. His philosophy as a manager seems to be to rule with an iron hand. He can "tear someone up good and seems to enjoy it."

B. *Pro*

1. Extremely sound technical person.
2. Effective decision maker. Usually, decisions are well thought out.
3. Very effective in carrying out organizing function of management.

Con

1. Manager's primary weakness is in the area of human relations. He has a real problem relating to his people and making them feel comfortable.
2. His people are reluctant to go to him with problems of any kind.
3. Many times it is not so much what he says but how he says it.

C. *Pro*

1. His major strength is that he is a good engineer and has a good mind.

2. When applied properly, his attention to detail is an asset.

3. If he can modify his attitude toward people, he has tremendous potential as a manager.

Con

1. Sometimes his desire for detail is unreasonable.

2. He delegates a project and then follows it up too much. He does not appear to trust people.

3. His allocation of assignments leaves much to be desired. Jobs are given from one person to another.

D. *Pro*

Well versed and educated in areas that require technical judgment.

Con

1. Problem in human relations. He does not have the knack of making you feel at ease. You do not know exactly where you stand with the boss.

2. He does not have the trust and confidence in the abilities of his subordinates to the extent he should based on the true abilities of his people.

E. *Pro*

Has a good mind.

Con

1. He is very weak in delegating responsibility.

2. He is somewhat two-faced about many of the things he does. He will present one side to his superior and peers and another to his subordinates. For example, he accepts criticism graciously, and then turns around and gives his people hell and accuses them of giving his department a bad name.

F. *Pro*

1. From a technical standpoint he is quite good.

2. He is well organized.

Con

1. He is somewhat arbitrary on trivial points.

2. He has difficulty in releasing control of projects.

3. He has a problem in dealing with people.
    a. He will talk with one person and get information and use this to booby-trap someone else.
    b. He needs to improve on being such a fault finder and his head-on approach in taking corrective action.

After reading the report the manager requests a counseling session. Although the report has shaken him somewhat, he seemingly is open minded as to how he might build on strengths and overcome weaknesses in the way he operates as a manager.

As consultant, what will be your objective in the counseling session? After determining your objectives and strategies, role-play this case with a member of the class appointed to play the role of the manager.

Case 17—ABC Division OD Case

Assume you have been called in as a consultant for the ABC division of the Milton Corporation. The ABC division consists of two plants involved in fabrication of metal buildings.

The general manager informs you that he is unhappy with the performance of the Indiana plant. The costs of fabrication are getting out of control and there has been high turnover among operative personnel. The general manager's office is located in the Iowa plant and this plant is doing fine.

You suggest to the general manager that you utilize an OD approach to identify problems that are preventing the plant from reaching its potential effectiveness. He agrees and you meet with all supervisors and foreman who comprise the middle and first-line management ranks. The organization chart of the plant is shown in Figure 27.

When meeting with the foremen and supervisors, you tell them the purpose of the meeting and ask them to respond confidentially to the following question: "What are the problems that are preventing this plant from reaching its potential effectiveness?"

The twelve people present write their answers and turn their cards in without signing their names. Based on the following inputs, what action steps would you recommend the plant take to deal with these problems? Write a consultant's report setting forth your recommendations.

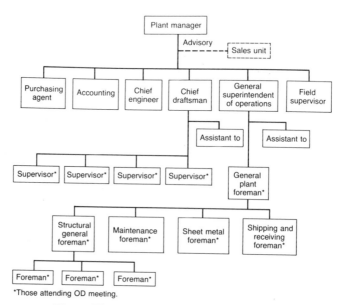

Figure 27. Organization chart of Indiana plant.

There were 64 specific problems identified by the group, and, of course, some were mentioned more than once. For example, seven people mentioned the problem of excessive overtime. After classifying the problems, you arrange them in the following categories: (1) supervision and leadership (mentioned twenty-four times), (2) communication (seventeen times), (3) pay and working conditions (eleven), (4) planning and organizing (six), and (5) attitude and morale (six).

Supervision and Leadership (mentioned twenty-four times)

1. The problem of the lack of improper delegation by managers, supervisors, and workers (mentioned seven times).
   a. After handling a problem and advising the supervisor, he then wants to get involved and often defeats my resolution.
   b. Lack of responsibility of many workers and supervisors.
   c. Not enough authority delegated.
   d. If a man is given a job to do let him do it. Don't do it for him.

e. Higher management always ready to jump on supervisors about problems without giving them a chance to work them out for themselves.

f. Lower managers have to do manual labor. Cannot supervise.

g. Foremen not allowed to do their jobs properly because some management thinks that they should be working at all times as well as supervising.

2. The problem of autocratic or authoritarian leadership on the part of some managers (six times).

a. One supervisor wants you to do as he says without any question whether its right or wrong. Just do it, damn it.

b. Supervisor: when you need to give a chewing out, should this be done in private instead of in front of your men?

c. One member of management that wears two faces. Does not work through supervisors.

d. The men are worked too many hours and expected to do the impossible at all times. This problem stems from one main source.

e. Ask and find the cause of errors before chewing the wrong man out when it may not be his fault.

f. Don't chew a man out in front of his men.

3. The problem of not practicing enlightened management that is taught in our management sessions and that we read about in management journals (three).

a. Why not practice what is preached?

b. These meetings seem to be talk and no do. We feel we should try to practice what is taught.

c. Talk about problems but never do anything about them.

4. The problem of favoritism (three).

a. Too much favoritism shown by management to certain individuals.

b. Some of our managers treat workers better than others because of social life.

c. Rules enforced by management for a small minority.

5. Faulty problem-solving (two).

a. Supervisor does not ask questions about problem and jumps the gun.

    b. Middle management trying to solve problems with workers without knowing anything about the problem. By this I mean a hasty decision that makes other employees mad besides the one with the problem.

6. Not working as a group (one).
7. Top management needs to improve in the way it operates things (one).
8. Middle management overruling lower management and not backing lower management in decisions (one).

Communications (seventeen times)

1. The problem of upward communications and reception of communication from lower levels (eight).
    a. No one in upper management to discuss a problem with.
    b. No one to represent a person and his problem.
    c. New ideas are not accepted openly.
    d. Supervisors not aware of all problems and when informed not doing anything about them.
    e. We have outdated ideas and one-way ideas that make up the way that our company is run.
    f. Top management should listen more to suggestions at lower levels.
    f. Cannot talk to higher management.
2. We feel we should have some say so at our plant, but everything has to come through our other plant; the theme here is "they do it this way in Iowa" (six).
    a. We have a communication gap from one plant to the other plant.
    b. Seven hundred mile communication gap.
3. The problem of downward communications (three).
    a. False or delayed promises.
    b. Employees need to be kept better informed of company plans.
    c. More honesty from management on individual's future.
4. The problem of communications in general (two).
    a. Poor lines of communication.

b. Management just needs to take more time to realize problems. And not pass them off as unimportant.

Pay and Working Conditions (eleven times)

1. The problem of excessive overtime; this implies that with proper planning and scheduling, there would not be a need for so much overtime (seven times).
2. The problem of pay (three).
   a. A definite need for a good incentive program.
   b. Wages.
   c. Slow raises.
3. Too much work in one day (one).

Planning and Organizing (six times)

1. Ineffective organization methods (one).
2. No organization in company (one).
3. Hard to schedule work as schedules change too often (one).
4. Need more planning (one).
5. We have the problem of controversy between some of our top managers; their goals seem entirely different, which creates confusion and dissatisfaction on every level (one).
6. Employees are kept under a strain and tension due to heavy work load and scheduling and lack of trained personnel (one).

Attitude and Morale (six times)

1. Morale very low (one).
2. Little respect for supervisors (one).
3. Higher management's attitude and behavior (one).
4. No respect for a person—treated as a machine (one).
5. Plant employees putting in extra hours because of errors of other people; this is hard for them to understand when they have already had a hard week (one).
6. Many supervisors are disgusted, thus hurting their effectiveness (one).

Index

370   60
450
200
540
─────
1560